Significant
Interiors

Significant Interiors

The American
Institute of
Architects

Diana M.H. Brenner, AIA, IIDA
Annie Chu, AIA
Timothy Hawk, AIA
Hank Hildebrandt, AIA
John G. Jessen, AIA, IIDA
Richard Logan, AIA, LEED AP
Kevin Sneed, AIA, IIDA, LEED AP

images
Publishing

AIA

Published in Australia in 2008 by
The Images Publishing Group Pty Ltd
ABN 89 059 734 431
6 Bastow Place, Mulgrave, Victoria 3170, Australia
Tel: +61 3 9561 5544 Fax: +61 3 9561 4860
books@imagespublishing.com
www.imagespublishing.com

National Library of Australia Cataloguing-in-Publication entry:
Significant interiors: the American Institute of Architects interior architecture
knowledge community.

Includes index.

ISBN 9781864702002 (hbk.).

1. Interior architecture – United States. 2. Interior
architecture – Awards – United States. 3. Interior
decoration – United States. 4. Architecture – United
States. I. American Institute of Architects. II. Title.

Coordinating editor: Andrew Hall

Designed by The Graphic Image Studio Pty Ltd, Mulgrave, Australia
www.tgis.com.au

Digital production by Splitting Image Colour Studio Pty Ltd, Australia

Printed by Paramount Printing Company Limited Hong Kong

IMAGES has included on its website a page for special notices in relation to this and our other
publications. Please visit www.imagespublishing.com.

Contents

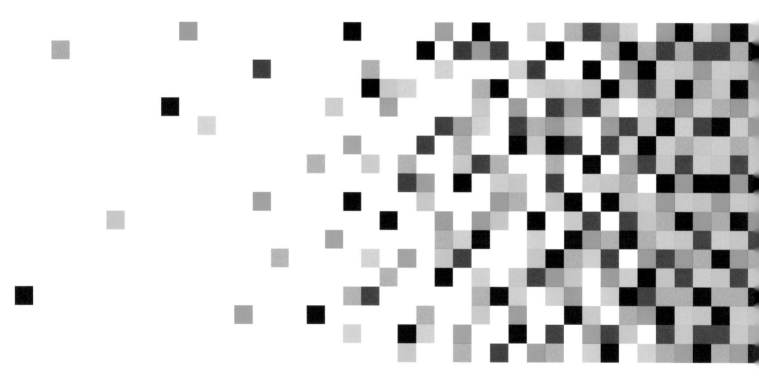

Foreword

The AIA Interior Architecture Knowledge Committee has discovered a wonderful way to express the diversity and creativity of interior projects generated through the 2000 to 2004 national AIA Honor Award programs. The result is a thought-provoking compendium of important design solutions that represents the best of interior architecture and demonstrates clearly that interior architecture is taking a place of importance in the world of design.

To their credit, the committee members used more important criteria than mere visual appeal in selecting projects to be featured in this book. They interviewed both the owners and the architects of the award-winning projects to gain an in-depth understanding of the critical factors involved in each solution. From this analysis, various "filters" emerged—Design Innovation, Inspiring Presentation, Creative Use of Technology, Exceptional Process Management, Social Responsiveness, and Client Satisfaction—which served as unique categories for discussing and evaluating the featured projects. Beyond serving as a structure for presenting the projects, the filters prove very revealing about what makes interior architecture meaningful. In each case, the projects shown in this collection go far beyond great aesthetics. They embody smart planning, creative use

of space, and imaginative use of materials that respond to specific programmatic and design needs and yield innovative interior architectural solutions. The committee members impart to readers specific points about each project that inform and educate us about the significance of the individual design solution.

In a nearly 50-year practice with a focus on interior architectural design, I have watched this area of the profession grow and evolve from a fledgling and fairly unimportant part of architecture practice to a creative, innovative, and significant component of the architectural process. The projects presented in this volume allow us to learn from the different ways users live and learn and, from the variety of forms created, to enrich their experience of these architectural spaces. Each example, in its own way, involves an extremely satisfied client who was stretched by the opportunity to participate in the project process and interact with the designer. The six filters provide a useful method for evaluating future interior architecture projects. By offering a greater understanding of what interior architectural design contributes, the filters can serve as a basis for not only future interior architecture design competitions, but also the way all design professionals develop their projects.

M. Arthur Gensler Jr., FAIA, FIIDA, RIBA

Preface

Since the late 1980s, the term "interior architecture" has been in use among practitioners and educators. The concept underwent a more formal treatment in *Interior Architecture* by John Kurtich and Garret Eakin, published in 1993. By 2003, the AIA Interior Architecture Knowledge Community (KC) had started to discuss the idea of creating a knowledge source about interior architecture. Although the AIA Honor Awards program began acknowledging significant interior work in 1993, profiles of the award winners had appeared only in *Architectural Record*; these articles, which focused mainly on design trends, did not address solutions beyond discussion of aesthetics. The committee considered these interior architecture design examples worthy of deeper study and analysis, which they felt could benefit the architecture community.

The Interior Architecture KC chose to base its book on the former Institute Honor Award for Interior Architecture winners, not only to document the award-winning projects, but also to analyze their significance and to offer more detailed information as to how the projects were conceived. The committee wanted to produce a reference for the practice of interior architecture that would give in-depth information about the projects, including recognition of interesting commonalities, contrasts, construction details, and other important facts. This type of book could educate architects about interior architecture, yet would appeal to other allied professionals and design educators.

The product of the committee's musings, this volume of *Significant Interiors* is intended to be the first in a series that will appear every five years as a retrospective of significant interior architecture projects, a sort of *Harvard Law Review* for interior architecture.

Diana M.H. Brenner, AIA, IIDA
Annie Chu, AIA
Timothy Hawk, AIA
Hank Hildebrandt, AIA
John G. Jessen, AIA, IIDA
Richard Logan, AIA, LEED AP
Kevin Sneed, AIA, IIDA, LEED AP

Introduction

Members of the American Institute of Architects active in the Interior Architecture Knowledge Community wanted to create a book that would identify interior architecture trends before they outlive their relevance. To accomplish this, the editorial team for this effort, made up of members of the knowledge community, elected to look at projects that had received the Institute Honor Award for Interior Architecture—specifically in the years 2000 through 2004. During this five-year period, the AIA honored 55 projects for excellence in interior architecture. The depth of coverage the editorial panel planned, however, dictated inclusion of a smaller selection.

Whittling down the number of projects involved examining copies of the original submission files, reading jury comments, and reviewing photographs and drawings for the 55 projects. Instead of re-judging the entries, a decision was made to establish a method for sorting and "qualifying" them according to why, and in what way, each was *significant* to interior architecture during the five-year period. The primary goal was to understand what made a project important beyond pure aesthetics and program function.

The first step was to identify the project types and client/user programs for the projects. This information provided a basis for the task of narrowing the number of projects to be profiled. As the panel catalogued the projects by standard categories—retail, institutional, hospitality, residential, and office/business—as well as by an organized year-to-year chronology, factors emerged for differentiating the projects.

Even before they had selected the 25 projects that proved most compelling, the authors realized that conventional methodologies for measuring design excellence seemed inadequate to establish the long-term significance of the award-winning work. Instead, the authors determined to identify what it was that made each project outstanding or differentiated it from typical work other than its function or exceptional beauty, fetching photography, or other aesthetic considerations. Some committee members had to overcome their preconception that award-winning work may not always represent lasting or significant advancement of the state of design, but rather represent mere stylistic trends.

The resulting evaluation effort proved both surprising and gratifying, as the committee members determined that each of the projects appeared to have significance for a broad range of reasons.

For some projects, innovation in design was clearly evident and compelling. For some, the presentation drawings were particularly captivating. For others, technological advancement was significant. Concepts that emerged from the projects—design *innovation*, inspiring *presentation*, creative use of *technology*, exceptional *process* management, social *responsiveness*, and client *satisfaction*—became "filters" through which the projects could be viewed. These filters helped the committee members differentiate the top 25 projects from the larger group. The shortlist they developed had a good cross-section of project types, as well as a reasonable spread of examples of all the filter categories.

All of the firms chosen for inclusion in the book were then asked to respond to a general questionnaire, which inquired how they thought their projects related to the filters. Each firm was asked to select one, two, and possibly three, criteria areas from the list of filters to describe their project. The editorial panel recognized that some firms had already done this to some degree in the narrative text included in their original award program submission. In this case, the firms were asked to re-examine their project, from both reflective and analytical viewpoints, and to write an in-depth assessment of it—with as many specifics as possible—to include in this publication.

The responses received from the firms were varied and sometimes unpredictable. Nonetheless, they were extremely helpful for ensuring the projects were being evaluated in the appropriate categories. After reading what the firms had to say, the committee moved some of the projects to a different filter category.

Members of the committee then divided the selected projects, and each person took responsibility for a certain number of projects, communicating with the design firms and preparing a written profile of each project. To accomplish this, committee members gathered information about the projects assigned to them. The goal was to obtain direct input from architects as well as from clients and users. In some cases, members of the panel visited the projects or talked to architects who had. Sometimes additional documentation or more specific drawing details and descriptions were requested from the design firms. During the writing process, panel members discussed each profile as a group, sometimes soliciting help from other members of the AIA Interior Architecture Knowledge Community.

Filters as Evaluation Tools

The editorial panel wanted to qualify the projects to be included in this work with a methodology grounded in a set of particular criteria. The idea was to look beyond the aesthetic design of the projects to factors such as technical details, trends, and functional considerations. The filters that were identified intentionally move away from the usual programmatic categories used to discuss architectural interiors. Each filter reveals one aspect of what makes interior architecture meaningful, including the qualities necessary to translate that meaning from idea to reality. By a process of consolidation and elimination, the six filters the committee arrived at were defined and more clearly refined. Then the projects were evaluated again to determine which filter seemed most appropriate for each. Multiple categories may have been relevant to one project, but for clarity, simplicity, and a certain symmetry, each project was evaluated and is discussed through the view of only one filter.

The panel sought to begin a discourse on what it is about an interior project—distinct from its concept—that establishes it as a product of professional practice. This helped to identify issues of significance and established boundaries for the text and illustrations. Thus, the filters serve as tools for examining and explaining a broad range of interior architectural topics and issues and for encouraging a rich dialogue about the significance of interior environments.

Design Innovation

The committee considered innovative design to be the art of developing fresh ideas by applying the unexpected in either new or existing settings while addressing programmatic needs and project conditions. In innovative interior architecture, the designer may combine a variety of interior elements and technologies in new ways. Such combinations synthesize elements of interior architecture (such as lighting and daylighting, form and composition, and spatial sequence), novel applications of materials and products, and unique space planning or program applications, transforming them into beautiful compositions.

Once a project was assigned to the design innovation category, the architecture firm for the project was asked to address the following questions:

- What were the special design characteristics of the project?

- What was achieved in innovation in aesthetics—color, space, surface, detail, materials?

- Did the design challenge preconceived ideas or provide innovative solutions to address the client's needs?

- How did the design solution relate to the client's identity and advance the client's ideas about interior environments?

- How did the project advance the client's purpose or enterprise?

- How did the design advance the profession's current design approach and aesthetic concepts?

Inspiring Presentation

How the architect communicates a design to the client, and other project team members, influences project development. In the review process, the committee looked at both the quality of the award submittals and the designer-to-user communication throughout the project delivery. The projects chosen to exemplify this filter exhibit inventive use of media and a quality of craft in the presentation of both detail and the formal design. The project designers also addressed the many levels of knowledge required by the parties collaborating on project delivery, most often through drawings and other pictorial images.

Each architecture firm with a project assigned to this filter was asked these questions:

- Which communication techniques were used in the design process?

- Which communication techniques and means were used in discussions with clients?

- Which advancements or unique graphic communication means (e.g., CAD models, animations, rapid prototyping, rendered perspectives, plans, and sections) were used in developing the project?

- How did written statements, beyond program documents, contribute to advancing design innovation and the conceptual understanding of the project—either within the firm or for the client?

Creative Use of Technology

This filter identifies how the architect used or developed technologies, whether new or established, to achieve unique results. Projects with special program requirements could be met with innovative uses of technology. Examples include building components that offer advanced technical developments in fabrication processes and building materials that may require specialized technical consulting. Projects in this category reflect the intelligence required to resolve their complex technical, structural, environmental, or other similar issues, as well as the program demands that led to solutions combining advanced technology with artistic expression and beauty.

For projects assigned to this filter, the firms responded to the following questions:

- How did the project further the development of interior technologies?

- Did the project advance the profession's understanding of specific technical components or areas (e.g., building systems, construction methods, and surfaces) used in interiors?

Exemplary Process Management

When a firm delivers successful design projects, little notice is usually given to the effectiveness of its project and process management or office operations or to advancements in delivering client satisfaction. Despite this, the ability to develop project programs into a needs-based design process that includes identification of strategic goals with measurable financial outcomes is a core value of professional design services. Successful projects require effective business organization and the ability to include the client in the design process. The process begins with determining at the outset what must be asked and measured throughout project delivery and after project completion to ensure the client's goals are met.

Each architecture firm with a project assigned to this filter was asked to further address the following specific questions about their project:

- What were the unique management processes or procedures and requirements the firm employed for the project?

- What were the unique management parameters for this project?

- Which in-house management processes did the firm use to develop and complete the project such as budget, man-hours, site conditions, or schedules?

- How was the project completed?

- What successful management aspects of this project has the firm been able to build on?

Social/Environmental Responsibility

The projects presented in this category demonstrate concern for the environment, ethical accountability, and the societal role of interior architecture. Discussions of the projects center on how interior architecture shapes spaces and benefits the way people live, learn, and fulfill their spiritual needs. The projects demonstrate how well thought out designs can integrate environmental issues and economic criteria to achieve quality design and advance professional ethical standards. They also acknowledge the need for professional accountability and the fact that environmentally responsive design is a holistic process that balances specific environmental responses with aesthetic demands and program requirements.

The firms responded to these additional questions about their projects:

- What significant advancement was made in health, safety, and welfare issues beyond required standards and codes?

- Did your firm consider following LEED or other Green Building Council criteria for the project?

- What contribution did the project make to the quality of life of the building users and immediate community?

- What advancements were made in sustainable design issues (e.g., environmentally preferable materials, indoor air quality, reuse of materials, and energy use)?

Client Satisfaction

Establishing strategic goals early and translating program requirements into the design solution initiates a needs-based design process that emphasizes evaluation of the completed project in terms of client/user benefits. This filter is intended to differentiate project effectiveness from client satisfaction within a project.

For a successful evidence-based evaluation, the client must commit to evaluation benchmarks and post-occupancy evaluation early in the design process to enable a complete information feedback loop. Strategic planning is crucial when setting goals and pinpointing areas for achievable success in a project. Expectations for each performance level are established, and the project delivery process is structured to produce specific outcomes according to these expectations. Quantifiable results from a project evaluation depend on collaborative participation and direct evaluation. Owner, architect, and users envision goals based on realistic success measures that reach beyond aesthetic accomplishments. Evaluation criteria draw from solutions as they are experienced over time, often long after the architect's involvement.

Criteria used for further evaluation of the projects assigned to this filter came from answers to these questions:

- Were any measurable evidence-based evaluation criteria put in place at the beginning of the project?

- Was there any quantifiable data collected to measure client satisfaction or goal achievement?

- Was a post-occupancy evaluation completed for the project, or any other consultant evaluation carried out, to assess effectiveness of the project design?

- Were any surveys, client testimonial letters, quotes, or comments collected after the completion of the project?

- Has the firm revisited the project to assess design objectives or put in place any systematic procedure to assess the effectiveness of design services?

Using the Filters to Evaluate Interior Architecture in a Historical Context

The filters developed by the AIA Interior Architecture editorial panel to analyze the projects in this book produced concepts that can be used to evaluate other interior architecture, as well. For example, the famous tent room (Zeltzimmer) in Prussian architect Karl Friedrich Schinkel's Charlottenhof villa (1826–27) can be viewed through the lens of several filters. Designed as a space for ladies-in-waiting, the tent room places an outdoor structure indoors, embodying the concept of an interior–exterior exchange. The design illustrates the concepts of *design innovation* and *inspiring presentation*. Schinkel used the "tent" element both literally and figuratively, with tent-like blue-and-white striped cotton fabric that invoked a feeling of being outdoors but at the same time secure indoors. This novel treatment of vernacular elements created symbolic and functional space; it was an innovative design presented in an inspiring way.

A century later, Le Corbusier interpreted program, landscape, and the "primal tent" in his Ronchamp pilgrimage chapel (1954–57). Like Schinkel but with different motive, Le Corbusier viewed landscape and architecture as conceptual principles; the chapel interior exploded with plastic space and light. Of the filters that could be used to examine the Ronchamp interior, Le Corbusier's *creative use of technology* was perhaps the most compelling. On the interior, the structural frame of the shell-like reinforced concrete ceiling is hidden, allowing the overhead sweep of the ceiling to continue past the wall to the exterior. This composition produces a thin band of daylight that washes through the glazing onto the textured ceiling surface, making the mass shell roof structure appear to float as if suspended by a higher power. Structural expression was manipulated to achieve lightness and spatial plasticity—a creative use of technology.

Shifting the discussion to modern times, Sam Mockbee made unique advancements in design services that improved the human condition and brought client satisfaction, which he viewed as the architect's responsibility. A clear connection to the *social responsibility* filter was evident in all the projects of Mockbee's Rural Studio, which he founded with D.K. Ruth in 1992. Beyond its many innovations in reuse of materials and unorthodox forms, Lucy's House is a good illustration of the Rural Studio's socially and environmentally conscious directives. The sleek, low roof pitch and horizontal "modernist" aesthetic of Lucy and Anderson Harris's house in rural Alabama displays several striking features, such as walls constructed of salvaged carpet samples. The nylon fiber and backing material of standard carpets are toxic landfill products that damage the environment, so finding ways to use them is an environmentally friendly action. Also important is the idea of taking the essential character of carpet—modular thicknesses and sizes; variations in color and texture; soft, acoustical, and thermal properties—and employing the carpet modules as if they were brick courses to form exterior and interior "soft" walls and partitions. This configuration extended the notion of accountability and material stewardship to artistic expression, which provided the Harris family not only with shelter but with a beautiful home. The Rural Studio projects demonstrate how interior architecture can effectively respond to the demands of social responsibility, ethical accountability, and the societal role of interior architecture in improving people's lives.

The principal idea behind standardized measures such as the filters in this book is that their use can give greater depth and meaning to the interior design of the last several years. It is hoped that these AIA Interior Architecture Honor Award winners from 2000 to 2004 will stimulate similar critical dialogue in the years to come.

Quantifying exemplary innovation in interior architecture is a difficult task. The ideas that constitute innovative design are subjective as they are rooted in our zeitgeist, the cultural context of the time in which they were designed. For the purposes of this book, however, innovation is invention, improvement, and a combined sense of risk and vision that yields an element of creative freshness and unique aesthetic advancement.

The projects that follow received AIA Interior awards from 2000 to 2004 and demonstrate a high degree of innovation and creativity. The four projects selected for discussion here—Fifth Avenue Duplex, Qiora Store & Spa, and Craft Restaurant, all in New York City, and Ackerman McQueen Advertising in Tulsa—are innovative on several levels.

Striking composition of interior space and creative application of materials and lighting unite these projects. The architects featured carefully chosen materials bathed in beautiful light and positioned in well-composed spatial volumes. Near-perfect still life compositions of volume, material, texture, and light project emotional tones that elevate, beyond expectations, the response to a potentially mundane design problem.

Innovation can be defined as a creative transformation sparked by re-examining known conditions, the outcome of which is often new trends and styles. This process can emanate from several creative energies and is often synthesized through collaboration. It seeks to balance technological adaptation and application—both old and new—with an understanding of beauty, all within the enterprise of efficiency and effectiveness of built work.

The criteria for what is innovative take into account contemporary notions of beauty—the formal aesthetic issues of composition, shape, and proportion—as well as traditional knowledge of form applied as balance, contour, mass/void relationships, proportion, foreground/background, and so on. Applying these viewpoints to a project often activates the interior environment because it turns everyday qualities into something outside the expected—a new frame of reference determined by clever compositional arrangements. Such compositions are visible, for example, in the reception space of the Ackerman McQueen Advertising Executive Office and Video conferencing project. A simple glass vase cradling an organic element—a branch—placed on the entry table in an axial

position appears as an object composed within the interior space defined by lighting, textures, and material. This ensemble brings together the aesthetic beauty of individual objects to energize a formal spatial composition.

Other less obvious, less formal criteria (such as spatial sequence, program content, and technical applications) are often at work in the effect of interior architecture as well. Subtle organization of spatial context and sequence within a plan, balance in the proportions of spaces, the use of natural light and lighting on materials and surfaces, and the poetic manipulation of materials and function add to the innovative energy of a design. For aesthetic effect, designers may combine such techniques by applying new technologies and new products that are tied to specific project requirements. Such combinations are celebrated as new product applications, new fabrication processes, or new expressions of form.

Significantly, each of these projects mirrors the client's enterprise. The Fifth Avenue Duplex in New York City allows the architect/owner to reference the historical context of prewar housing, which contrasts with the use of functional expression and

formal composition of space and volume. In the Craft Restaurant, culinary skill is mimicked in the craft of the interior architecture. For the Ackerman McQueen Advertising project, the architect animates the urban context through transparent blue light that represents the theater of video imaging. Qiora Store & Spa amplifies the beauty of products by using light and translucent organza fabric, which provides seclusion in a temporal environment.

In their clear sense of freshness, these projects embody innovation. Each achieves unexpected and lyrical results by combining standard compositional tools with unique products and materials and applying them in spectacular ways. All of the work has reached a level of expression, beauty, and art that is worthy of note, demonstrating that the art of aesthetics is also the art of interiors, whether the architect's innovation results in an extraordinarily functional plan, wonderful use of materials, or a set of beautiful details carried throughout the work.

Design Innovation

In the Box

Ackerman McQueen Advertising Executive Office and Videoconferencing, Tulsa, Oklahoma

Elliott + Associates Architects

The Ackerman McQueen advertising agency is housed in a 1917 downtown Tulsa office tower that features 18-foot ceilings, massive concrete columns and cross-braces, and dramatic skylights. In their 1999 design for a new videoconference center on the first floor of the building, the architects developed an "in the box" design concept. Their design showcases a transparent theater of moving images that plays with light and shadow and reflects the client's emphasis on imagery and media.

Ackerman McQueen believes that showing great work in a great space is critical to the quality of the videoconference experience for the firm and its clients. With this in mind, the architects created a sense of tension, movement, and stimulation in the videoconferencing center space. Natural light and artificial light function as insight and idea, making light the medium that defines the space and reflects the work of Ackerman McQueen.

The design carefully orchestrates space and light to evoke a feeling of movement and liquidity. A glowing "blue box" of moving images serves the large videoconference room, small videoconference room, AV technical area, and corridor. Light is brought into the space with a shadow catcher, in which the captured sunlight turns passersby into moving silhouettes. For the people inside, the effect is that of a full-size motion picture.

A public corridor runs through the space, with offices, conference rooms, and a cyclorama on one side and a library and additional offices on the other. A transparent blue box—the heart of Ackerman McQueen—is in the middle. In it, the line between inside and outside, observer and participant, is deliberately blurred. People outside the box resemble an audience at a movie, while those inside become actors in a creative drama. The space is kinetic and atmospheric, with light entering through clerestories and from towers and from rope-like filaments hanging from ceiling fixtures.

The deep blue colors used throughout the space are meant to create the feeling of being in a television studio, or "blue box," to further emphasize the link between the client's business—advertising—and the design of the Ackerman McQueen offices. In creating an environment akin to a production studio for the videoconferencing center, the architects acknowledge the function that media and information play in the client's purpose and how they affect the final advertising message. Light, shadow, and movement combine to paint a three-dimensional portrait of a company on the cutting edge of 21st-century communications.

Opposite:
Main entry

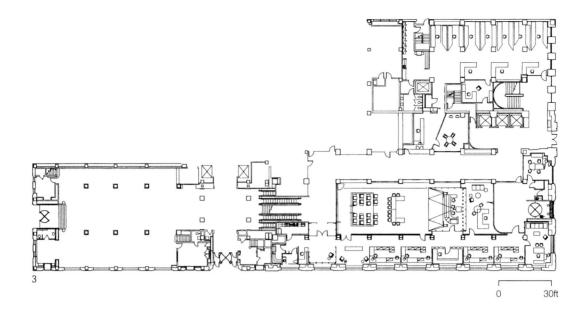

3

0   30ft

4

5

Opposite:
Reception looking south
3   Floor plan
4   320 South Boston Building, Tulsa
5   Blue glass detail at east window

6

7

8

9

10

6   Video conferencing space "Blue Box" (preset mode)
7   Video conferencing space with screens illuminated
8   AV room
9   Executive office Blue Box detail
10 Executive office view of Blue Box

11

12

13

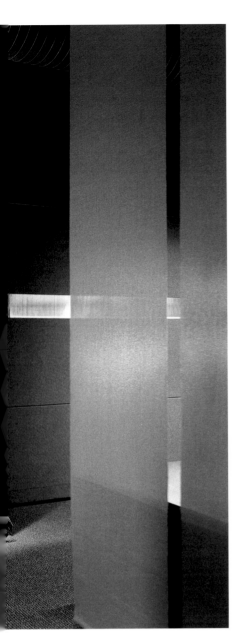

14

11 North–south walkway looking south at work station
12 Steel column detail
13 The only remaining original building plaster cornice
14 Revolving door dressing room
15 North–south walkway looking north

15

Not a Shout, but a Whisper
Fifth Avenue Duplex, New York, New York

Shelton, Mindel & Associates

This duplex with Central Park views offers a study in contrasts and contradictions. It juxtaposes old and new, matches strong solids with playful voids, and achieves both formality and informality. Using a range of design innovations, the architects have intermingled disparate elements in a masterful and calming composition.

Creating a living space from a pair of Manhattan flats is hardly a unique problem for designers, but they rarely get the opportunity to tackle double-high spaces and create a very private individual residence. In this instance, the architects have surpassed the task of providing a pleasant living environment for a sophisticated client. Developing spaces that have meaning beyond the obvious, they have successfully interwoven a number of themes—history, functional expression, and volume and space—into their finely crafted design. As well, the use of light and materials elicits subtle responses to these interiors.

Renovations of this type often ignore the building exterior. Here, the architects take into account the historic nature of the structure. The inside face of the narrow street façade, with tall, elegant, historically significant windows, is treated with traditional wood-paneled cladding similar to that often found in buildings of the prewar era. The detail is repeated on freestanding columns elsewhere in the space. A sweeping, curved stairway with traditional balusters graces the entry space. All of the historic and historically influenced woodwork has a white lacquered finish that plays subtly against the all-white finishes throughout the formal living and dining spaces. The design infers that this charming old building deserves respect, even when its intent is to create clean, minimalist spaces within.

Functional expression is another theme the architects take up. A long block of service elements, including stairs, kitchen, restrooms, and the building elevator, runs the length of the unit on both floors. The long wall, clad in massive limestone blocks that clearly demarcate the core, is visible from almost every room. The strength of the limestone gives gravity and grounding to the spaces, and its strength is evident throughout.

The third story focuses on the rare opportunity to express interior volumes. The architects were able to capture the height of the space offered by the vertical adjacency of the flats in several places. The stairways float in open two-story volumes, and a double-height sitting area near the entrance overlooks the master bedroom suite. This use of space gives the duplex the feel of a private residence, despite its location in an apartment building.

The architects continue to play with functional expression in the use of materials, which change enough to prompt different emotional responses throughout, yet never veer far from a unified theme. As the spaces progress from the pristine, all-white formality of the living and dining areas toward the kitchen and its casual seating area, the materials become more friendly and warm. The reference to traditional details found at the front of the house disappears entirely in the more casual spaces. Wood cabinetry in the pantry, as well as kitchen and sculptural wood shelving interlaced with the limestone wall, penetrates the interior, and the transformation culminates in a shimmering metallic spiral stairway at the far end of the kitchen.

Sometimes expressive, often virtually invisible, lighting plays a supporting but critical role in the simple interiors. A glowing metal form, suspended above the high bay of the seating area off the living room, makes for a symmetrical and serene space, even encouraging a sense of the sacred. An irregular pattern of recessed miniature lights casts a mysterious glow on the variety of rich surfaces. The lighting concepts and the natural daylight that floods the interior from all sides reveal the sculptural qualities of the spaces.

Furnishings further support the play on contrasts. Although most of the pieces are modern classics from the likes of Bertoia, and Charles and Ray Eames, a few strategically placed transitional pieces add character and variety.

In these spaces, the power of architecture is evident throughout. With a nod to its historic envelope, a clear evocation of living functions, and a sculptural expression of volume in a quiet and respectful composition, this unusual duplex communicates with equal clarity in a whisper or a shout.

Opposite:
    East view of living room from entry

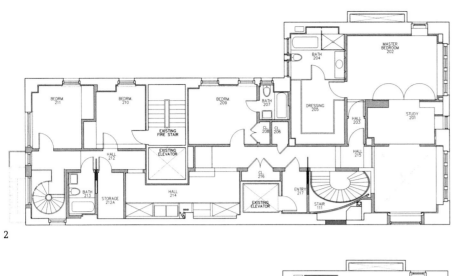

2

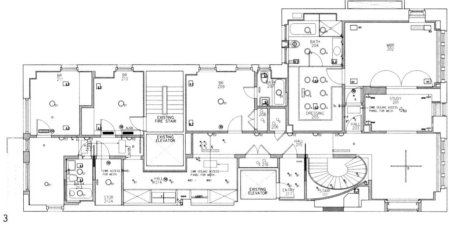

3

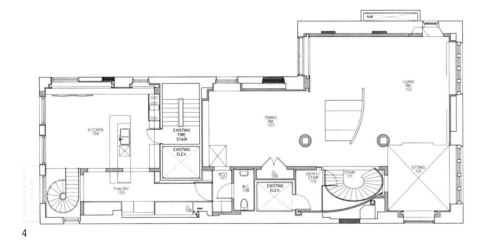

4

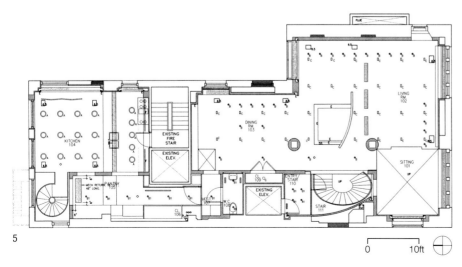

5

0   10ft

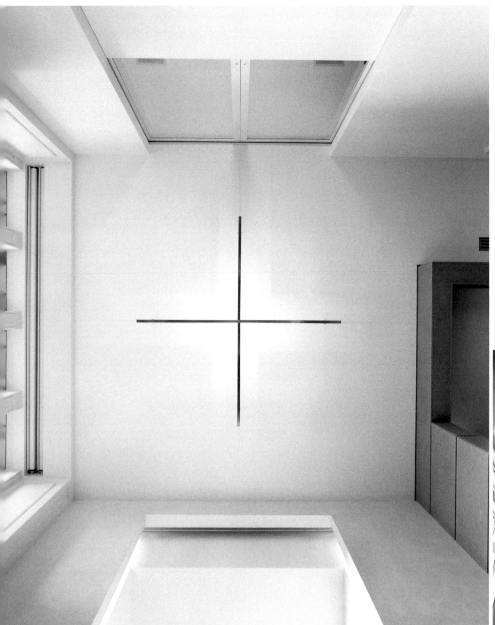

6

7

8

2   Construction plan – 11th floor
3   Reflected ceiling plan – 11th floor
4   Tenth floor construction plan
5   Tenth floor reflected ceiling plan
6   View of custom light fixtures at sitting room ceiling
7   Sitting room from master study above
8   Sitting room with view west to Central Park

9

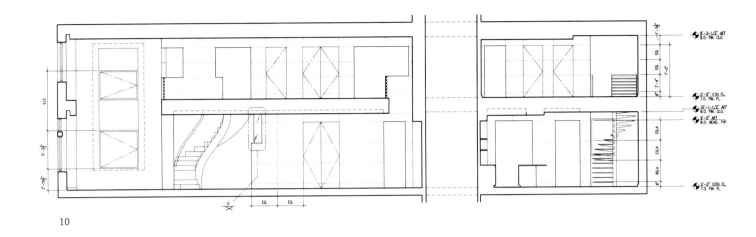

10

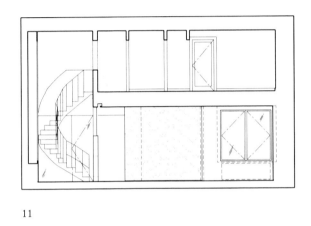

11

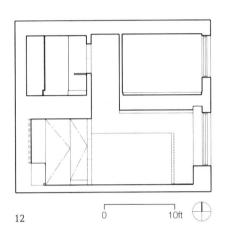

12

0   10ft

13

14

15

16

17

18

15 Master study from master bedroom looking west toward Central Park
16 Media area looking north with view to dining room beyond
17 Master bathroom
18 Kitchen facing east

Which Craft?

Craft Restaurant, New York, New York

Bentel & Bentel, Architects/Planners, LLP

Culinary craftsmanship is the chef's ability to portray cooking as a craft, rather than an art. According to the design team the restaurant's purpose is to "explore the full flavor of each artisanally raised ingredient on the seasonal menu, and serve these unadorned creations on separate plates placed at the center of each table for all to share." Craft Restaurant not only celebrates special food and service, it showcases the process of design and the craft of the laborers who are responsible for creating this texture-rich and spatially impressive interior. So how can you determine which craft is which? Where does one craft end and the other begin? The project is an exploration of the ingredients, the contrasts, and the spice. The restaurant draws on the patron's appreciation of the space, the food, and the atmosphere created by the union of the many crafts needed to accomplish a common goal.

This intimate restaurant was conceived from the gutted wreck of a department store built in 1886 in central Manhattan. The 130-seat restaurant and bar of 5,425 square feet includes a 2,200-square-foot kitchen and a 3,500-bottle wine storage area. The entire operation occupies the first floor and cellar. The chef's simple approach to food inspired the architect to experiment with a limited set of finish materials and to employ straightforward, high-quality craftsmanship to join them.

Five distinct elements define the restaurant space: a highly customized steel and bronze wine vault, a curved walnut and leather-upholstered paneled wall, a space-expanding mural triptych, terra-cotta-clad columns preserved from the original space, and amber-hued bare-bulb lighting elements. The long (80-foot), narrow space has a 14-foot-high ceiling clad with wood-fiber ceiling panels. The room is spatially compressed and then released by the juxtaposition of the curved, paneled wall against the mezzanine-height wine vault. Each old and new building element exhibits a connection between its form and its structure and, at the same time, easily relates the scale of the room overall to that of the human body. The result is a comforting and comfortable space.

Each element in the interior was carefully designed and executed. In particular, the custom-created wine vault is a collaboration between designer and craftsperson. Its design required a high level of detailing, combining wire mesh, steel plates, and bronze bars. The bar top is slightly oxidized steel that has been waxed: its patina is from use in the ironmonger's studio, where the wine wall and bar were built.

The leather-paneled wall is made of vegetable-tanned calf leather normally used as a bookbinding material. The designers chose this type of leather for its tactile qualities—it was crafted to be held in the hand. The leather was carefully seamed and stitched to create a sculptural relief of form and pattern, and the resulting wall curves along its length and slopes inward at the ceiling. Even the simple fasteners, washers, and screws holding the leather panels in place were installed with skill and care. To understand the fabrication issues posed by their design, the architect made full-scale mock-ups of the panels and experimented with them in the office. The resulting wall provides a warm, rich backdrop along one edge of the room.

The "temperature" of materials was also considered by the architect. The cool steel and bronze of the wine rack contrast with the warm feel of the leather panels. Even the perceived heat from the bare filament light bulbs contrasts with the cold clay columns. All of the furnishings and fittings, including the cherry dining tables and bronze bathroom sinks and hardware, were designed by the architect to further refine the character of the restaurant. Using only beeswax to protect the natural materials, the designers intended for the furnishings and fittings to gain patina and age gracefully.

The design solution combines such elements as space, form, color, materials, and textures to create a three-dimensional composition that reflects the soul of the client's enterprise. The success of the final design is a result of the careful collaboration of the architect, chef, artist, and craftspeople who engaged in a compelling process that resulted in an enduring and artful work of architecture.

Opposite:
View of bar, under wine vault balcony

2

3

2 Existing storefront condition
3 View from the street looking through original storefront window
4 Sections
5 View from maitre d' stand at front looking toward rear
6 Detail of seating area under wine vault balcony at rear

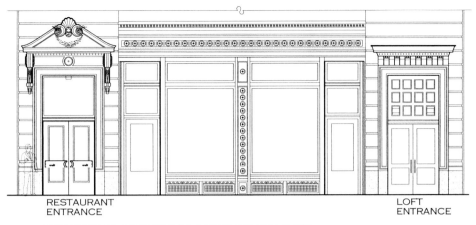

RESTAURANT
ENTRANCE

LOFT
ENTRANCE

STREET ELEVATION (REFURBISHED)

SCALE: 1/8" = 1'

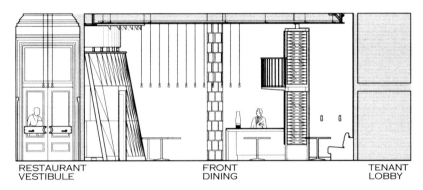

RESTAURANT
VESTIBULE

FRONT
DINING

TENANT
LOBBY

SECTION A-A

SCALE: 1/8" = 1'

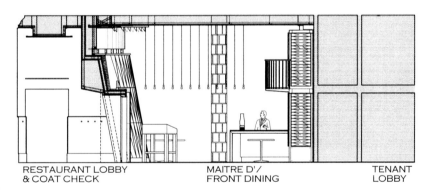

RESTAURANT LOBBY
& COAT CHECK

MAITRE D'/
FRONT DINING

TENANT
LOBBY

4

5

6

7

8

1   Entry vestibule
2   Coats
3   Front dining
4   Bar
5   Bar dining
6   Rear dining
7   Waiter's station
8   Restroom
9   Stair to kitchen
10 Stair to upper wine rack

7   View of alcove dining at front of restaurant
8   Detail of bronze column "capital" and terra cotta column
9   Floor plan
10 View of bar dining looking toward mural at rear
11 View from rear dining area, looking at wine vault

9

0   10ft

10

11

12

13

12 Detail of leather-paneled wall
13 Detail of wine slings
14 Close up of wine vault
15 Rear dining area showing mural at left
    and salvaged brick wall
16 View from wine balcony toward rear

14

15

16

Rhapsody in Blue
Qiora Store & Spa, New York, New York

Architecture Research Office, LLC

Diffused lighting emits a luminous glow on transparent fabric panels and flows through these curvaceous forms at Shiseido Cosmetics' Qiora Store & Spa in New York City. In this Madison Avenue salon, the first space in North America dedicated solely to Shiseido's new line of skin care products, Architecture Research Office (ARO) fused product and space to offer customers a sensory experience emblematic of Shiseido.

This innovative interior satisfied current "branding" elements by blending the product directly into the interior space. Unfortunately it was only a temporary prototype to be used for other shops/salons in the United States.

At the store entrance, massive windows afford passersby clear sightlines to the interior, where curvilinear shapes encourage exploration. Products sit on glowing display fixtures illuminated with fiber-optic uplighting that cycles through shades of white during the day and aqua in the evening. For soft boundaries around the retail consultation and reception areas, the designers chose suspended, translucent organza fabric panels. The layers of veils, tinted in shades of aqua or milky white and suspended from the ceiling, become denser as you move toward the back of the 1,500-square-foot boutique. In the spa, fabric shrouds the more intimate lounge and cabin areas, where Ultrasuede lines the opaque walls.

Qiora's interior environment reveals its design innovation; it amplifies the product offerings and preserves the openness of the boutique for retail customers, yet creates intimate spaces for spa clients. The designers achieved this effect through an innovative use of fabric and light. Round spa cabins, articulated by translucent organza fabric, provide a feeling of seclusion within while maintaining the openness of the store throughout. Another inventive design element is the spa cabins that are placed in the midst of the retail space. Instead of isolating spa and retail offerings, the designers manipulated light and material for the kind of atmosphere that would work for each of these two disparate user groups—spa and retail. The retail environment was reconceived as a calm, metaphorical outdoor space. The outer edges of the spa cabins create a curvilinear surface, which augments the experience of visitors to the store, encouraging them to explore a unique setting.

To preserve this sense of openness, the service rooms are located along the south edge of the boutique. Storage areas and office space are below street level.

The designers incorporated an intense use of light to conceive, study, and present the design. From early studies through the initial client presentation, they employed a light table to build project models so they could visualize and contemplate the effect light could have on the space. Subsequently, as the project developed, they created a full-size mockup of the lighting to test the spacing of light fixtures and the filtering of the fabric shades.

The design achieves an innovative use of light and materials: warm- and cool-temperature fluorescent light fixtures at the store's perimeter emit light that changes the lighting mood and proportion. Unlike the distracting track or recessed fixtures typical in most stores, the boutique has a pleasing glow on the interior that enhances the product display. As a space-enclosing element, the use of fabric eliminates distracting seams, supports, and other elements. Strips of custom-dyed organza fabric hang from the ceiling and are stretched tight by the weight of metal bars that slip into sleeves in the bottom of each strip.

The client wanted the store to act as a beacon for the introduction of its products. The design is a physical elaboration of the products' qualities providing the sensory experience of being outdoors. Starting with this idea, the emerging language of forms, materials, and lighting creates a warm, glowing landscape that is visually open to the exterior. Light is the primary material of the interior.

Located at the front of the store, the retail area presents small groupings of the product, whose elegant packaging lends color, scale, and detail to the space. The day spa, which has three massage cabins, a lounge, showers, and changing areas, is situated at the rear. The 20-foot-high ceiling and the large windows establish an open, expansive atmosphere that supports the entire design strategy. Curvilinear shapes maximize the perceived size of the boutique and create a continuity of space that encourages customers to explore the entire interior. Three cylindrical spa cabins float in plan, blurring the boundary between the retail and spa areas.

Opposite:
    View of the store exterior at night from across Madison Avenue

The floor is white poured epoxy, a seamless reflective surface that enhances the overall glow. As visitors circulate through the space, layers of fabric panels continually reconfigure collages of color and light. In the spa, fabric shrouds the more intimate spaces of the lounge and cabins. The walls of the cabins are opaque and lined with Ultrasuede, creating a soft and quiet place for relaxation. The shower floors and walls are clad in large sheets of warm white acrylic.

Transparent blue hues and lights, along undulating curves within a moderate-sized space, produce an impressive design whose innovations with light and materials work well. This gradual transformation of light changes how one perceives the space over time, reinforcing its connection to the outdoors. The Qiora Store & Spa provides a rhythm to the space that expresses enthusiasm.

2   Floor plan
3   View of the consultation spaces
4   Detail of spa cabin interior, with Ultrasuede and organza walls
5   View of the main interior space

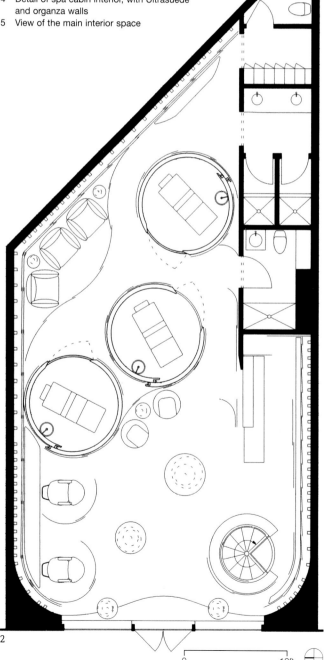

2

3

4

0   10ft

5

7

8

9

Opposite:
  Detail of resin product shelves
7 Table with product containers on a foreground shelf
8 Detail of table with shelves in the background
9 Sketch of the main interior space

Design presentations document the story of a project as it evolves from concept through construction. Presentations translate abstract notions of parti, special functional relationships, materials, and light into an explicit description of the desired experience and spirit of place that form the aspirations of the client and intentions of the designer. Presentation media and methods are the designer's tools for storytelling. Presentation was selected as a filter for critical review in this book because it is through the designer's presentation that the story of a project and its place is understood. As exemplified here, this storytelling tool enables recognition of certain designs with an AIA Honor Award.

The projects showcased in this chapter were selected for review as outstanding examples of storytelling through the designer's use of available tools—text, design process images, constructed and virtual models, and photography—that clearly demonstrate how the project design objectives were achieved and the design problem resolved.

Morphosis used three-dimensional imaging technology to develop its design for Lutèce, a restaurant in Las Vegas. The committee felt the firm's exceptional use of technology distinguished its presentations and clearly explained the complex relationships of space, form, light, and material through each phase of the design process. The design team described its concept through a series of three-dimensional, computer-generated sketches and models that explain the experience of patrons as they pass through the narrow passages that dramatically open onto the intimate dining room. Photographs of the completed project effectively describe the spatial relationships as well as the details that thoughtfully complete the design.

Robert M. Gurney used a different approach in working with his clients on the design of their Washington, D.C. home. For the Fitch O'Rourke residence, Gurney had the benefit of the clients' expectations for a "modern interior" through a written design brief. The design was developed through extensive meetings with the clients as more than 50 models were constructed to help them

understand the articulate interrelationship of forms and arrangement of the interior spaces. The photography of the built project provides dramatic views of the elegant design solution; from interior to exterior, and public to private, spaces; and from spatial volumes to intimate details.

To illustrate their design for the Pallotta TeamWorks National Headquarters in Los Angeles, architect Clive Wilkinson and his team referenced the expressive drawings generated by Christo in his *Blue Tents* proposal, to demonstrate the communicative potential of such emotionally charged sketches. With their broad strokes and striking colors and textures, sketches of this type may appear childlike, but the addition of crisp detailed sections and plans fleshes out the powerful themes of material and form in the architects' interior design. The resulting graphic communication package exhibits the creative design process and metaphoric inspiration, but also mirrors the client's intrinsic attitudes: participatory, informal, and resourceful.

In each of these project presentations, the designer used a variety of media and methods to express the design intent of the project. Whether using computer-generated imaging technology or handcrafted physical models, the designer's tools give the viewer a three-dimensional experience of the spatial relationships of the interior. Written descriptions translate the client's aspirations into design principles used to guide the designer and client through the design process. These presentations provide the viewer with an understanding of how the designer achieved the client's aspirations through the design solution. Evidence of the success of the design is indicated in the photographs of completed projects, which use broad views to clarify the design concept and overall organization of the space, and intimate views to clarify how conceptual materials and details carry through to the final resolution of the design.

Inspiring Presentation

Oasis

Lutèce, Las Vegas, Nevada

Morphosis

A serene respite from the cacophonous interior of the Venetian Casino, Lutèce is a quiet, calm oasis in the Las Vegas casino environment. Building on the reputation of a successful sister establishment in New York City, the restaurant serves French cuisine in what is intended as a refuge for weary, hungry, and thirsty nomads in the gaming desert.

The interior of the restaurant is visually interesting and restful. On entering, customers pass through a bronze portal etched with a conceptual plan of the restaurant—a hint of things to come. The floor is supported by a sculptural installation by artist Do-Ho Suh that is so subtle it almost appears as a texture on the floor. As explained by the architects: "Once inside, an army of tiny sculpted figures, with arms raised above their heads, supports the elliptical glass floor beneath the guest's feet. The sculpture contains 19,000 human figures, equivalent to the entire population of the casino resort at a given point in time." A massive wine wall is reflected in the curved glass walls of the main entry, creating the illusion of a space of much larger scale. The wine rack defines the curved perimeter of the bar area, and serves as a light trail directing customers into the main dining areas.

The architecture of the interior appears formed as if by centripetal force, orbiting the main dining room. The design was conceived as architecture of chance, with origins in the roulette wheel and bouncing ball, the most basic symbols of Las Vegas games. Morphosis describes the segments of curved wall as seeming "to spin about their off-center axis as irregular cutouts, which perforate the drum form and reveal views of adjacent spaces."

Rather than creating visual confusion, the overlapping, connected spaces in the restaurant elicit a calm response. Perhaps it is the simple palette of color and materials that lends a sense of quiet. The space is a play on contrast: dark bronze bands against white drywall and smooth, curved, transparent walls against the jagged sculptural solids. According to Morphosis: "The geometry emanates from an abstraction of the classical formal dining room, finding its focal point in the massive chandelier above the main dining space." The dining room is encased by a white, bronze-banded wall, in the form of a conical ellipse, which wraps the room and functions as the key organizational gesture, creating a sense of movement between areas.

The same material evolves with a fluidity of form that mediates the transition into the remaining spaces. Encircling the main dining area is the reception area, bar, wine storage, patio, and private dining room. The feeling is almost one of a tent in the desert, with a sense that a sweeping wind surrounds it.

Only one small area is open to an outside terrace and seating area. The restaurant generally focuses inward, ignoring exterior views of the Venetian's Grand Canal and ornate décor.

The restaurant's lighting enhances the atmosphere of the space. With light sources cleverly hidden, the only identifiable fixture is that of the chandelier element, yet the lighting clearly distinguishes the abstract forms and walls, revealing the true texture and color of the materials.

The way a design is presented to a client or an awards jury can be as important as the design itself. Strong verbal communication and evocative drawings can give a client a preview of how users will perceive the final design. In the case of Lutèce, the visuals—two-dimensional graphics in plan and three-dimensional images in axonometric drawings—served the architect well in describing the proposed design intent. Simple parti diagrams and line drawings potently expressed the dynamic nature of the design solution. Like visions from a mirage, the architect created an illusion of the desired effect.

For an entry in a juried design competition, a minimalist approach and a presentation with visual strength are key. Strong visuals allow the team to document the design with fewer words. The architects who designed Lutèce used an unveiling montage to present beautiful drawings coupled with artfully composed photographs to tell the story of the project. The composition leads the eye from wide-angle views to miniscule details.

Lutèce presents itself as a contemporary interpretation of a classic culinary force. The architecture has taken an awkwardly shaped space and brought to it a sense of order, scale, and balance. The result is indeed an oasis from the intentionally insular, disquieting casino environment, and its design acts as both a foil and a reference to the frenetic air of chance and motion. The architect's presentation of the project is as compelling as the final product; it allows the viewer to comprehend the concept and enjoy the journey.

1 View of dining room
2 Dining room detail
3 Sections

1

2

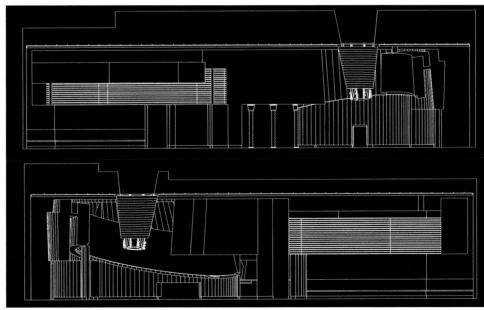

3

4

4 Floor designed by artist Do-Ho Suh
5 Dining room detail
6&7 Main entry

5

6

7

Presentation Quality
Fitch-O'Rourke Residence, Washington, D.C.

Robert M. Gurney, FAIA

A vaguely Tudor-style row house in Washington, D.C. is not normally the type of residence that inspires awards from the American Institute of Architects. But this renovated living space is a rare and exquisite exception—rare, because few residential projects have so thoroughly changed the character of the original structure while maintaining a respect for it; exquisite, because the design is superb and remarkably consistent.

Yet, for all its architectural bravura, this project was selected for the Presentation filter because its unique spatial qualities were beautifully rendered in presentation drawings and models, and because the clients were unusually explicit in their direction to the architect. The kind of space that was constructed could only have resulted from either a very sophisticated client or a very persuasive architect—and this project had both.

The interior build-out of this four-level structure stemmed from a near-fiasco in its historic neighborhood, when a developer—intending to convert it to condominiums—partially gutted the townhouse. Since this charming district had always been devoted to single-family homes, the city put a stop to the multi-family proposal. The property was abandoned and allowed to decay for years; the problem being how to create a functioning residence out of its hollow shell.

No one could see its potential until the current owners discovered the property. The husband's father had been an architect, and the couple envisioned a thoroughly modern home within the historic shell. Evaluating costs and potential salvage, they planned to completely demolish the internal structure, preserving only the front facade and party walls.

The clients were remarkably clear about their intentions for the house. They contributed uniquely to the process of design and gave the architect all the direction he needed to attack the problem of designing for a wonderfully sophisticated, yet demanding client pair. In a written brief that describes their vision of a modern interior, they made their desires clear by emphasizing what they didn't want:

"By Modern, we don't mean the kind of safe, boring, architecturally sterile, contemporary interior design ethic of a typical new home in [the suburbs]. We don't mean the type of obsolete 1970's or 1980's

Modernism with clunky roof beams and big round windows. We also don't mean the 1980's Modernism of extreme minimalism and endless white walls. We don't want a temple to sheetrock, and we don't mean the equally obsolete postmodern style with ornamental columns, Palladian windows, and dorky oversized dormers. You don't need an architect for that."

Instead, the clients interpreted their vision for the contemporary house: "cutting-edge, architecturally innovative Modernism" that seizes the opportunity to create something new. "The result should be sophisticated and inventive with elements that are unexpected, gutsy, and perhaps even fun and playful. The design should be something that fulfills our functional requirements, but which you as an architect would like to see written up in professional magazines … feel free to consider use of adventurous materials, brightly painted surfaces, oblique walls, and asymmetric spaces."

With such an edict from a client, which architect wouldn't be ready for the challenge of his/her career—especially in Washington, a city of normally very conservative tastes? Remarkably, considering the confines of a historically significant structure, the final result turned out to be all that the clients had envisioned.

In a typical design approach for a row house, the architect would line up rooms along its length. Instead, the design of this house focuses on a range of spatial experiences produced from complex geometric expressions. The geometry is composed of two simple elements—a curve from the front to the back of the house, and a 10 percent tilted axis of all the internal spaces. These two devices lead to an amazing variety of spaces, and with some of the floors removed to create open segments and triangular voids, the internal volumes became a kaleidoscope of rich forms.

The exquisite shapes, volumes, and juxtaposition of materials, while complex in their execution, create a surprisingly comprehensive composition—an interior that is warm and comfortable, yet bold and expressive. Concrete, wood, and metal play off one another with confident gusto.

Although the results look effortless and intuitive, achieving them posed a challenge. How did the architect create such a remarkable interior with the consensus of the clients when they had set out such

Opposite:
View from second floor toward the main entry

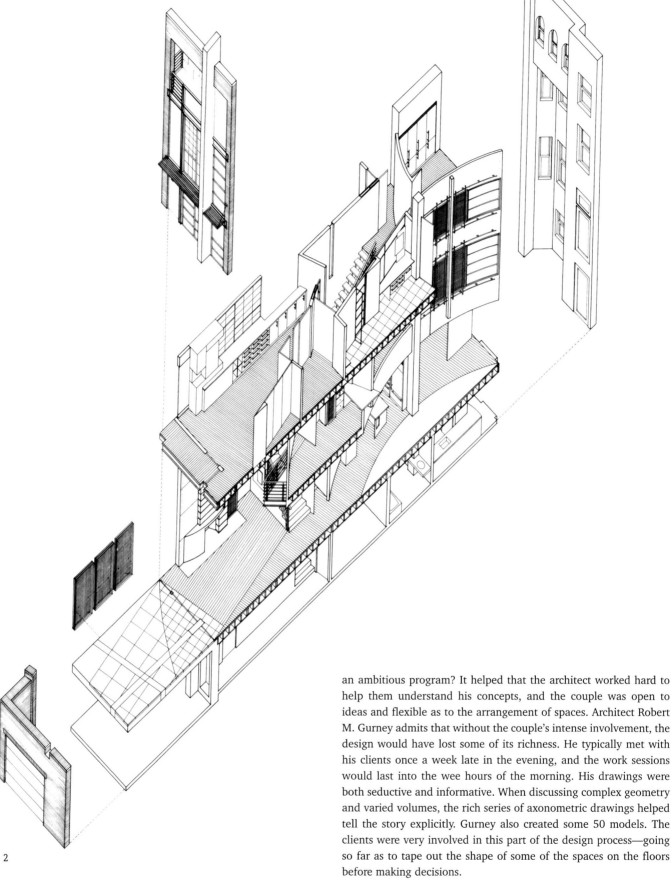

2

2 Exploded axonometric
3 Living room looking north

an ambitious program? It helped that the architect worked hard to help them understand his concepts, and the couple was open to ideas and flexible as to the arrangement of spaces. Architect Robert M. Gurney admits that without the couple's intense involvement, the design would have lost some of its richness. He typically met with his clients once a week late in the evening, and the work sessions would last into the wee hours of the morning. His drawings were both seductive and informative. When discussing complex geometry and varied volumes, the rich series of axonometric drawings helped tell the story explicitly. Gurney also created some 50 models. The clients were very involved in this part of the design process—going so far as to tape out the shape of some of the spaces on the floors before making decisions.

"We believed Modern architecture could be warm and good looking, as functional as traditional design, and achieved at a moderate cost," one of the clients explained. They were right, and the richness of the presentation process, along with their intense involvement in it, ensured that their dream was realized.

3

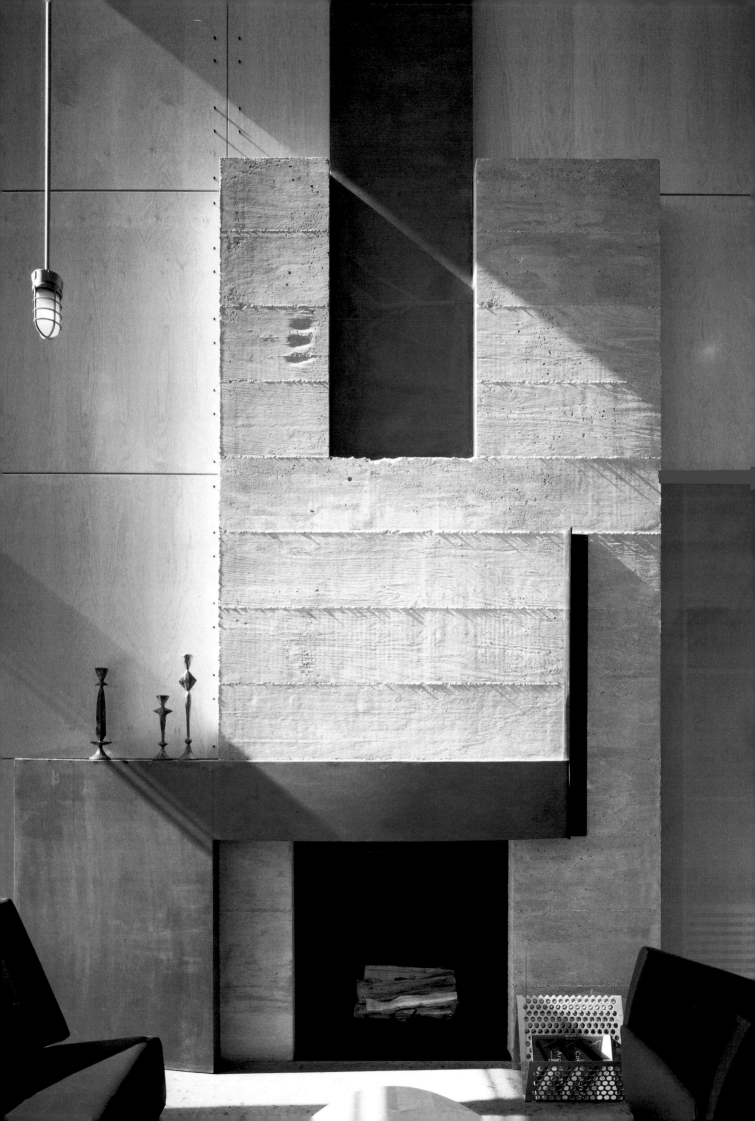

5

6

Opposite:
View toward the living room fireplace
5   Living room looking south
6   View looking up into skylight

The Medium is the Message

Pallotta TeamWorks National Headquarters, Los Angeles, California

Clive Wilkinson Architects, Inc.

The mobile "tent cities" created by charity event company Pallotta TeamWorks to house participants at fundraising activities became the inspirational beginning for the design of its new national headquarters. To be located in a large warehouse, ubiquitous in Los Angeles, the facility became an ideal structure for moving the "tents" inside to create office "neighborhoods." The limited budget forced architect and client to interface the indoor tent concept with program requirements and evolve other creative approaches for the headquarters design. The result was fresh design solutions represented through artful presentation techniques that drew from the surrounding industrial vernacular of the location, as well as from the Los Angeles area's energetic graphic attitude. Large "breathing tented islands" were conceived to divide the work environment into smaller identifiable neighborhoods and minimize the heating/cooling footprint of the space.

The 47,000-square-foot unconditioned warehouse structure provided an ample two-story floor-to-roof height in which the architects could develop numerous tent islands. This concept helped overcome the tight budget by reducing investment costs in mechanical equipment and lowering energy costs by reducing lighting, cooling, and heating loads. The architects were able to develop a lively office environment and build on the client's beliefs in environmental responsibility and sustainable policies. Staff members would spend most of their time in the neighborhood tents, permitting localized controlled environments to minimize air conditioning and energy use but still fulfill program needs.

For the architect, the tent island concept translated Christo and Jeanne-Claude's playful 1984 *Blue Tents* sculpture into office neighborhoods organized according to programmatic needs. The tent-like structures were created from standardized shipping containers placed within the warehouse landscape and modified from their original prefabricated narrow shape to accommodate conference rooms, office work bays, or textured backdrops for signage and graphics. Each container is extended with raw plywood-and-stud bay window additions.

The arrangement of containers, which serves as a spatial enclosure and portal, offers stimulating elevation compositions of stacked "tents" juxtaposed against other vernacular building materials. The

placement of the tents results in dynamic "spaces within a space" that are linked providing a visually rich sequence of internal streets, paths, and corridors. Large cutouts in the industrial corrugated containers restructure their spatial proportions and allow indoors to spill out via standard patio doors. The corrugated containers are painted with saturated primary hues of blue and orange that contrast with the exposed plywood-and-stud construction. All this stands under a canopy of sleek tent fabric that diffuses Southern California's natural light.

Shapes, volumes, colors, textures, and raw industrial materials combine to elevate the client's themes with animated design statements that interpret "familiar" building materials in new ways. Reflecting the ever-changing California design zeitgeist, this palette of material expressionism is placed in the *Presentation* filter category based on the architects' graphic presentation of their submission and their innovative design solution.

Architect Clive Wilkinson and his team referenced Christo's *Blue Tents* installation as a metaphor for the planning process and model of human intervention to help realize the client's vision. But it is Christo's expressive drawings, generated for his *Blue Tents* proposal, that show the potential of emotionally charged sketches to communicate powerful themes of material and form. These sketches often appear childlike, with broad strokes and striking colors and textures, but Christo often supports his work with machine-quality drafted and dimensioned drawings to complete his presentation package. This approach parallels the formatted submission for the Pallotta project, in which simple informal line sketches were mixed with cryptic notes, symbols, and exploded diagrammatic images. Crisp detailed sections and plan drawings accompanied these sketches to present process content and thematic expression.

The graphic communication package for the Pallotta headquarters not only exhibits the creative design process and metaphoric inspiration, but also mirrors the client's intrinsic attitudes of participation, informality, and resourcefulness. The complexity of the program is graphically described and technical energy-saving innovations are communicated with the combination of visual note sketches and scaled measured drawings. Casual freehand and diagrammatic sections and oblique cartoon-like views project the

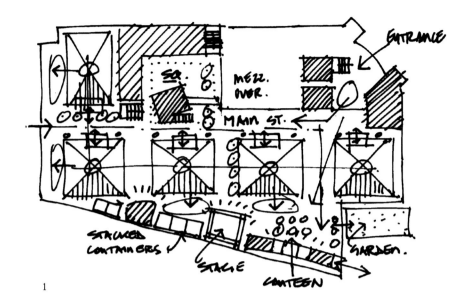

1

2

3

4

1 Concept plan
2 Exposed wood framing on new walls at the edit suite
3 Sleeping tents at a client's charity event
4 Christo's Installation of *Blue Tents* in Japan, 1984–91

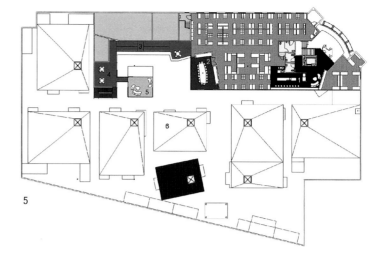

1 Break area
2 Conference room
3 Ramp
4 Meeting area
5 Brainstorming room
6 Tent

5

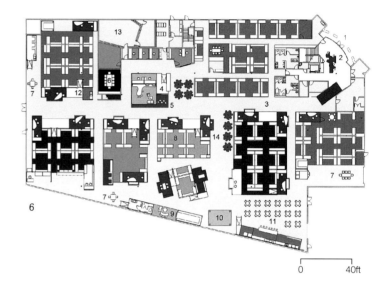

1   Main entrance
2   Reception area
3   Main street
4   Container tower
5   Reflecting pool
6   Conference room
7   Informal meeting
8   Work area
9   Lounge
10 Stage
11 Cafe
12 Pantry
13 Studio
14 Container

6

0   40ft

informal nature of the client's working style and the intended direction of the Pallotta program. Digital modeling and precision CAD orthographic drawings supplement these drawing techniques. The result gives a clear understanding of process, idea, and solution to the 47,000 square feet of office workspace.

In typical upfront Southern California style, the architects' felt-tip pen illustrations also communicate the fluid relationship between client and architect. The interior architecture uses exposed plywood and stud construction, tent fabric, bar joist, and shipping containers to translate Pallotta's brand image into a casual and relaxed work atmosphere. The materials produced to illustrate the project demonstrate quality communication media, themed intentions, and a presentation that is one with the built product.

The playful and inspiring interiors of Pallotta TeamWorks' new head-quarters present the client as a dynamic and responsible company that validates the popular axiom "the medium is the message."

7

8

5&6　Floor plan
　7　Container office
　8　View of stacked containers
　9　Interior detail
　10　Cafe formed of three containers

The bitterest tears shed over graves are for words left unsaid and deeds left undone.

HARRIET BEECHER STOWE

9

10

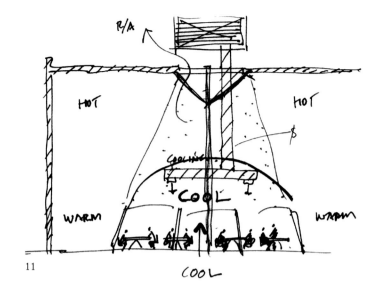

11

11&17   Tent concept sketches
  12   Interior detail
  13   Meeting room
  14   Work station
  15   Reception desk based on Buckminster Fuller's Dymaxion Map
  16   Floor detail
  18   Main Street

12

13

14

15

16

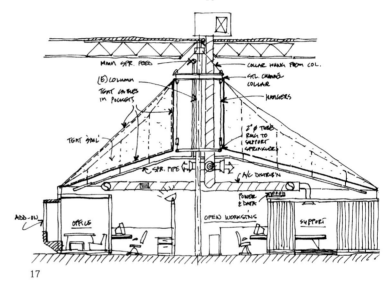

17

18

Measures of design excellence take many forms—the extraordinary application of technology to achieve a unique purpose is one. The five projects selected under this category have solved technical problems in unusual ways, without sacrificing the artistry of the design.

From the almost-invisible new lighting system at the New York Public Library to the unbelievably light structure for the new International Terminal at the San Francisco International Airport, which spans a whole roadway system, these examples of great architecture seamlessly integrate technology and structure, and simply express how things are made.

Researching the technical qualities of past AIA Interior Award recipients, the team asked the architects a number of questions about advancements they made in solving technical issues on the projects:

- In what ways did the projects further the development of interior technologies?

- Through which specific technical components or areas did the project advance the profession's understanding of interior technologies (e.g., building systems, construction methods, materials and surface treatments, fabrication processes, detailing and casegoods, lighting, acoustics, indoor air quality, ergonomics, wayfinding, and so on)?

- Which specialized technical consultants or tools were used (e.g., specialized CAD programs) to develop the project?

- Which technical advancements did the firm make use of on later projects?

Although most respondents chose to enter their projects in the more esoteric award categories of design or cultural advancement, the committee felt a number of projects contributed to the advancement of technology—even when the architects were unwilling to make such claims. They were, in some cases, too modest.

The five projects described in this chapter are culturally significant, thought-provoking, and beautiful, but they are also intelligent expressions of how elegant solutions to technical issues can contribute to the art of architecture.

A remarkable loft in the middle of SoHo in New York City, designed by the Architecture Research Office, features a pair of stairways that appear to defy gravity. For all their structural bravura, however, they derive an unquestionable beauty from a sense of logic that is not immediately obvious.

The massive new International Terminal at San Francisco International Airport—designed by Skidmore, Owings & Merrill (SOM), San Francisco, in association with several other firms—is a showcase for an amazing collection of technical achievements, from its massive span of almost 400 feet to its climate-controlled housing of precious artworks. Despite all the technical issues that had to be solved, the building seems light and almost effortless—an intuitive collection of structural and other design solutions that are beautiful, in part, because they are so apparent.

Another project celebrated for its technical achievement is the New York Stock Exchange trading floor, also by Skidmore, Owings & Merrill. Technical gadgets that enhance the process of trading fill the new trading floor, yet they succeed because the design was based on how the traders actually use the space. The architects analyzed the traders' activities and addressed them as if the traders were anthropological subjects. Their frenetic habits and use of technology during the trading day were subjected to close scrutiny. The analysis of the observed activities was used to develop a design that works— the space addresses the traders' unique work patterns, and it derives its beauty from its expression of their requirements for movement and access as well as for visibility and function.

The masterful restoration of the exquisite Rose Main Reading Room at the historic New York Public Library, planned by Davis Brody Bond, was executed with restraint and reverence for the elements of the historical design. The architects managed the insertion of up-to-date technological systems—vastly enhanced lighting systems, current computer technology and electronic media, and improved air circulation—into an historically significant space with extraordinary finesse, retaining and even enhancing the beauty of the space.

The offices for CoOp Editorial in Santa Monica, California, designed by Pugh + Scarpa, offered an unusual opportunity for that firm to create new interiors in a building designed by another well-known architect—Frank Gehry. The interior is defined by a sculptural wall of laminated timber, which is in turn offset by a series of laminated Plexiglass cubes that enclose workspaces. These deceptively simple forms, made from seemingly ordinary materials, are in fact a complex series of assemblies made possible only with the use of digital and laser technologies. Despite this complexity, the final result is wonderfully lyrical and fresh.

The designers of all of the projects in this chapter have addressed significant technical issues with resourcefulness and intelligence. Each architect has no doubt achieved technical advancement, but the greatest measure of their accomplishments is exhibited in the poetry and beauty of their work. There can indeed be art in technical advancement.

Creative Use of Technology

Structural Virtuosity

SoHo Loft, New York, New York

Architecture Research Office

Sunlight and soaring space characterize this timeless 7,000-square-foot, two-story loft in a former SoHo warehouse in Manhattan, but it is the technical wizardry of its elegant stairways that sets it apart.

With a rare location that allows access to light and views in all directions, the loft organizes spaces by relating them directly to the position of the sun. Bedrooms face east for the morning wake-up call, living spaces are oriented to the west, a library is washed in diffused northern light, and the double-height circulation space is flooded with light from a massive, translucent skylight. While almost all of the spaces have exterior windows—large punched openings in the 19th-century façade—most of the loft's interior is illuminated by etched-glass partitions that surround the main stairwell below the skylight.

More than half the loft's space is contained in one large open area, where most of the building perimeter is visible. The composition creates a grand space for entertaining large groups and more intimate areas that are subtly differentiated by etched-glass screens, millwork islands, distinct materials, and the sculptural stairs. In fact, the loft is almost entirely free of interior walls, except those between bedrooms and at the bathroom core. Another exception is the massive, blue Bahia granite-clad wall that separates the kitchen from the main space and provides a brilliant splash of color. The intense blue of the stone is repeated in the furnishings, and area rugs intensify the soft green tint of the etched glass and skylight to enliven the otherwise neutral palette.

The diffused light that permeates the spaces gives the loft its gracious, alluring presence, and is accented throughout with detailing that is clean and forthright. The highly articulated stairways punctuate the spaces like jewelry on a fine costume. Their beauty is derived from their pure, albeit surprising, structural expression.

A focal point in the loft between the living and dining areas, the floating, glass-supported stair to the roof terrace, has a see-through structure that maintains the visual continuity of the main floor. Designed and developed with structural engineers Guy Nordenson

Associates, it is a grand sculptural piece that appears to defy gravity. A floor-to-ceiling sheet of 1.5-inch-thick laminated glass is the physical support for a series of stainless steel tubes that serve as risers. Milled aluminum U-brackets and subtreads made from aluminum plates fasten and connect the elements, and solid oak planks form the surface of the treads. The tubular risers are connected to the glass with brackets and each rests on the riser below for support at the outer edge of the stairway.

Structural cascading supports the stair as the load is transferred from riser to riser via the aluminum plates that support the treads. The cascading support counters and disperses the stresses on the glass, allowing it to be thinner than expected. However, because the forces that accumulate at the bottom of the stair are so great that the glass would shatter, the last riser sits on the floor and does not engage the glass plane. Computer models were used to determine the stresses on the glass and steel tubes and plates. What appears to be an impossible structure is quite stable and sound.

Even the single, sweeping handrail that spans the entire stair height appears to be supported by magical forces. The often limiting code requirement for 4-inch spacing of balusters is met by thin cables strung like harp strings between the handrail and the risers. The entire effect is both disquieting and poetic.

A second stair, though somewhat more conventional, is equally beautiful. Constructed of a thin folded-steel plate over an amazingly thin steel stringer, the stair has treads and risers clad in solid oak planks and a repeat of the harp-string baluster design. This stairway, which connects both living levels with the roof terrace, exhibits a unique grace in its appearance as a silhouette against a glowing, backlit wall of etched glass, sitting in profound contrast to the massive granite wall by the dining area.

The entire SoHo loft features a sensible arrangement of functional and gracious living spaces, but it derives its unique quality from the quiet play of sunlight against simple architectural forms, enriched by a series of awe-inspiring structural expressions made possible through an unusual use of materials and construction.

Opposite:
Lightwell on the seventh floor

3

Opposite:
    Detail of glass stair with risers
3   Construction detail of glass stair
4   Detail from below the glass stair
5   Glass stair handrail detail

4

5

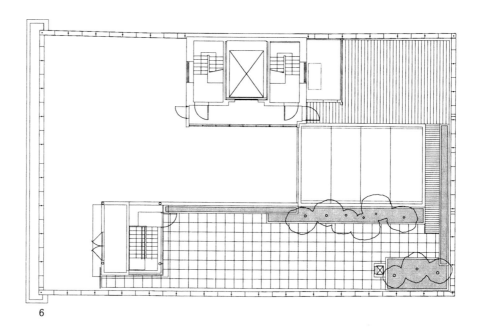

6

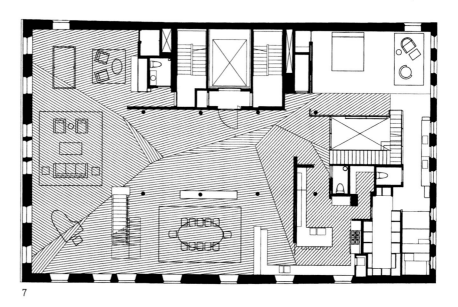

7

6   Roof plan
7   Seventh floor plan
8   Sixth floor plan
9   View of the seventh floor
10   Kitchen
11   Detail of slate shutter in the bathroom

8

0   10ft

9

10

11

12 Lightwell from below
13 View of the blue Bahia wall on the seventh floor
14 Stair and blackened steel wall

12

13

14

Technical Wonder, Work of Art

International Terminal at the San Francisco International Airport, California

Skidmore, Owings & Merrill, LLP

The new International Terminal at the San Francisco International Airport is the centerpiece of the airport's $2.8-billion expansion program. Designed to increase the efficiency and capacity of international arrivals and departures, the terminal gives the airport a strong, unifying public identity as the gateway to the city and the world. Skidmore, Owings & Merrill executed the competition-winning design for the terminal in joint venture with Del Campo Mauro and Michael Willis Associates. The technical achievements the design team reached in creating such a complex facility are both profound and beautiful.

The 2-million-square-foot terminal is essentially a multi-modal transportation facility that not only receives aircraft, private cars, taxis, and buses, but also hosts the Bay Area Rapid Transit (BART) rail system and an internal automated light-rail system. At five levels, the building is the first mid-rise terminal in the United States. Its vertical organization separates the various land transportation modes, making them easier to access for travelers, whether they are arriving or departing.

Chief among the new terminal's many technical achievements is its span of the airport's historic entry road. The site is essentially defined by the air-rights over the surface entry roads, which had to operate continuously during and after construction. This characteristic of the site, along with its prominence at the entry to the entire airport, were major influences on the unique design of the terminal. Another determining influence was San Francisco's desire to reinforce its position as America's gateway to Asia. In addition, the city wanted the airport to function as the hub of its transportation infrastructure. Accommodating such a variety of factors challenged the architects, who also wanted to go beyond a state-of-the-art transportation facility to make the terminal a venue for art and culture as well.

Given these complex requirements, the form of the terminal was generated by functional demands, but the architects were able to enrich the space with the qualities of light and lightness. Seemingly in contradiction are the need for a massive structure to span 400 feet across the entry road and the desire to let natural light define the public's arrival and departure experience. The building enclosure that resulted, however, is as much an instrument for admitting light as it is a barrier against the elements. At the same time, the structure conveys the building's role as a transportation center, as well as symbolically expressing its civic aspirations.

The architects achieved this design with two sets of double-cantilevered roof trusses that flank the airport's entry road and together carry a third set of three-dimensional, pin-connected bowstring trusses that complete the center span of the roof. The curved upper and lower cords of the structural members precisely trace the compressive and tensile forces residing in their long-span moment diagram. The 1,200-foot-long roof, with its gently rolling form, both reflects the Bay Area's natural rolling topography and expresses a lightness associated with aircraft construction. The terminal was also placed on friction-pendulum base isolators, allowing it to withstand powerful earthquake loads and function as an emergency center for the city following a 1,000-year earthquake.

The roof was conceived as a simple steel membrane stretched across the structure, unencumbered with lighting, mechanical, or fire-protection systems. With thin strips of glass separating the main trusses, the roof is the principal source of light for the building's public spaces. Significantly reducing the need for artificial light, it is the terminal's most visible emblem of efforts to incorporate environmental sustainability into the project.

Additional sustainable strategies employed in the building are among the designers' significant technical achievements. Ventilation using unchilled outside air is introduced near the floor, cooling only the occupied strata of public space. A 100-foot-long screen wall, constructed of wood harvested through certified sustainable forestry techniques, provides acoustical and visual screening between public and private spaces. As well, a linear natural bamboo grove planted in the main hall diffuses sunlight penetrating the terminal's western glass façade. According to the architects, the new terminal's architecture was developed in much the same way an aircraft might be designed, its form and aesthetics growing directly from functional necessity. The architects sought to distill the building to its architectural and structural essence. They obviously succeeded. With all its technical structural wizardry, the building clearly announces its purpose with an artful and elegant execution.

Opposite:
Detail of 3-D bowstring truss in the Departures Hall

3 Detail of the common-use ticket counter
4 View of common-use ticket counters
5 Exploded axonometric

The presence of art in public buildings has a long tradition in San Francisco and the way that the architects incorporated art in this project is an equally compelling technical achievement. From the beginning, the team took the position that art should be an important element in the design. For example, New York sculptor James Carpenter was commissioned to develop a series of cloud-like, translucent tensile structures that, through the use of dichroic glass panels, diffuse the light from the glass slots in the departure hall roof and highlight the structural frame's unfolding silhouette as the sun moves across the sky.

Beyond the artful expression of the building design, a substantial budget was allocated for art throughout the new terminal. The architectural team designed display areas to accept traveling museum exhibits, including vitrines and display casework with integral environmental and security controls. These installations are technically sophisticated pieces of product design with independent humidity, temperature, and lighting levels appropriate for the objects displayed. Because of the level of natural light in the display areas, clear ultraviolet-screening glass was used to protect works on paper. The designers placed these exhibition areas to encourage optimal public engagement. The displays are woven into the most active public circulation paths, making encounters with art and cultural artifacts a natural—in fact, unavoidable—condition of the travel experience.

The designers of the airport terminal solved many technical challenges with grace and ingenuity—no mean achievement. Yet beyond a mere technological wonder, the new International Terminal at the San Francisco International Airport is a symbolic gateway, a transportation hub, a crucible for art and culture, and clearly a work of art in its own right.

3

4

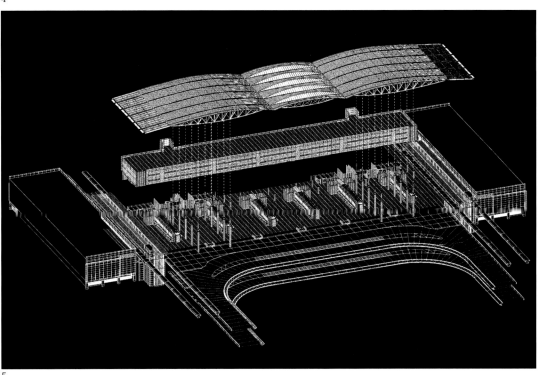

5

6

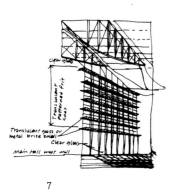

7

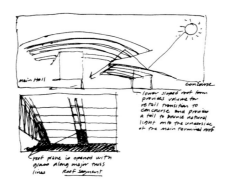

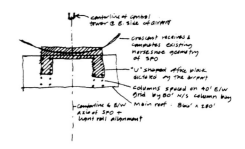

6 View of the west façade
7 Concept sketches
8 Roof truss computer model
9 Pedestrian bridge at the main entry

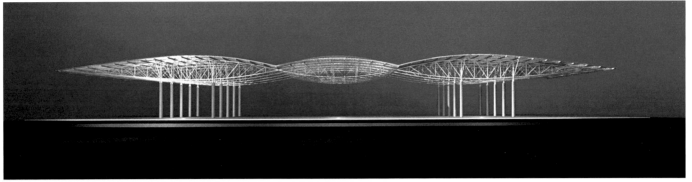

8

9

10

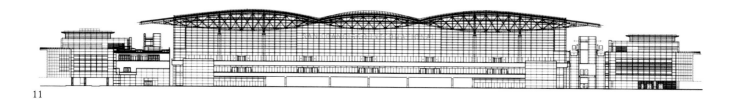

11

10 Night view of the west façade
11 West elevation
12 Concept sketch
13 Exterior view of the double cantilever roof form

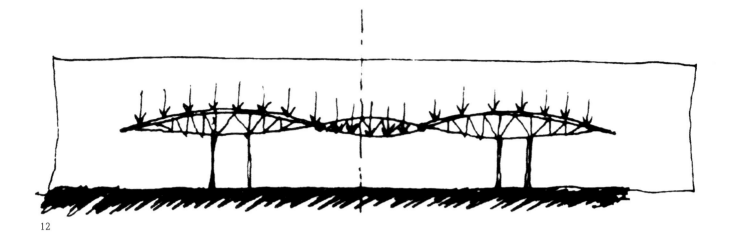

12

13

Trading Spaces

New York Stock Exchange Trading Floor Expansion, New York, New York

Skidmore, Owings & Merrill, LLP

The New York Stock Exchange, with its jostling, bellowing throngs of traders, is a study in human behavior at its most elemental. Commissioned to expand the trading floor, Skidmore, Owings & Merrill borrowed a page from Margaret Mead and treated the traders like anthropological subjects. The architects observed how the traders move "in incredible physical proximity to one another and the way they use different technologies, from phones and stock tickers to computers," explained one architect on the project. From their observations, the design team identified issues that should be addressed in its design for the space.

The architects faced a daunting task. In addition to designing a durable, technologically up-to-date, and user-friendly facility that could help stock traders be more efficient, they also had to give a world-renowned institution a contemporary makeover. The 43,000-square-foot trading floor expansion had to maximize the number of trading posts and larger training booths. Because the traders move closely and quickly around each other, the workspace had to be obstacle-free and made of durable materials that could withstand daily use.

While the architects worked out a design solution, they had the traders test full-scale mock-ups of new trading post designs. This research provided the architect and consultants with invaluable input. Using motorized systems to provide access allowed for flush installation of large rear-projection screens at perimeter walls, a must in view of the limited trading floor footprint. Another space saver was the use of architecturally exposed structural steel as frames to support monitors and canopies, which eliminated the need for cladding materials. Impact-resistant materials, and glass-reinforced plastic work surfaces, which create a shell appearance on the highly durable curved edges, provide comfort for users.

One feature of the trading floor couldn't be changed—the famous din. "Traders use the noise level to judge the markets," explains a design team member. "If it's too quiet, they get nervous." In fact, the electronics needed to keep all this activity flowing were a significant aspect of the redesign for the trading floor. After the opening bell, traders must have access to the technology that powers the exchange—a failure could be catastrophic. To respond to this need, the architects used vertical banks reached via mezzanine to elevate cables and hardware out of the fray. In addition, walls and bridge floors were used in lieu of traditional raised floor and ceiling cavities. The architects worked with manufacturers and designers of large display screens to achieve frameless, multi-ganged screens while maintaining the access requirements (such as three-minute maintenance rules) demanded by the NYSE's Security Industry Automation Corporation.

These concerns distinguish the redesigned trading floor from its previous incarnation. Work posts for specific industries accommodate more than one trader and feature pivoting flat-screen monitors mounted on a metal framework. Different kinds of information are packaged for easy viewing. General market levels, for example, are centralized on one huge screen above the main corridor, whereas company statistics show up on groups of nine flat-screen monitors canted above workstations.

According to the jury, the year this project won an AIA Honor Award for Interior Architecture: "The architect's total understanding and appreciation of the owner's complex program created order out of chaos and a fusion of architecture and the information age." The technical advancements achieved in this project have since become standard practice for projects of this type and have been used to engender a sense of excitement in many high-tech interiors.

1   View from level three
2   The ceiling along the arterial circulation is a series of modeled and folded plates

1

2

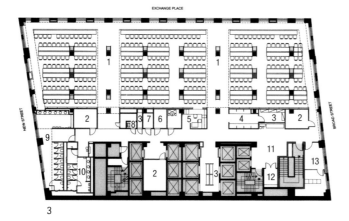

3

1	Trading post
2	Mechanical room
3	Storage
4	Coat room
5	Supervisor
6	Electrical room
7	Building electrical
8	Janitor's closet
9	Women's toilet
10	Men's toilet
11	Lobby
12	Waste room
13	SIAC

4

1	Mechanical room
2	Electrical battery
3	UPS
4	Plenum
5	Central distribution
6	Work room
7	Telephones
8	Men's toilet
9	Janitor's closet
10	Women's toilet
11	Coats

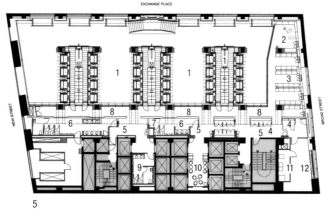

5

1	Catwalk
2	Interview
3	Booths
4	Closet
5	Vestibule
6	Men's toilet
7	Janitor's closet
8	Observation
9	Women's toilet
10	Lounge
11	Rack room
12	Media room

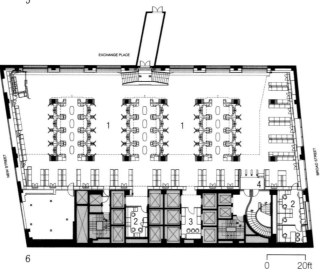

6

1	Trading
2	Floor operations
3	SIAC
4	Security

0   20ft

7

3 Level five (post-trading) floor plan
4 Level four (trading support) floor plan
5 Level three (mezzanine) floor plan
6 Level two floor plan
7 View of posts
8 View past post 20 to the manager's desk

8

9

10

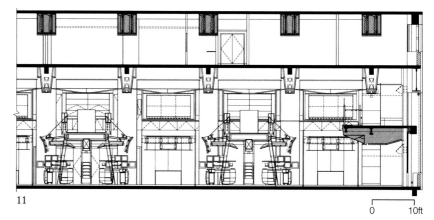

11

0   10ft

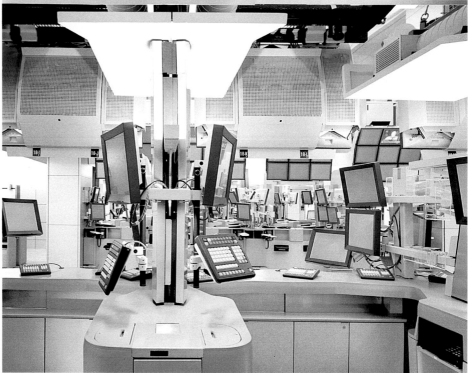

12

13

The Bloom is Back on the Rose

Rose Main Reading Room, New York Public Library, New York, New York

Davis Brody Bond, LLP

The New York Public Library—designed by Carrère & Hastings and completed in 1911—is a classical building with a unique plan inspired by the library's first director, Dr. John Shaw Billings. To maximize access to light and air, Dr. Billings placed the monumental reading room on the top floor, directly above eight levels of book stacks. Over the years, the original space for readers had diminished as other functions, such as copy services, microform readers, and card stack storage, encroached. Layers of dirt, water damage, and heavy use eventually dulled the aesthetic character of the famous reading room.

The New York Public Library prides itself on providing unparalleled public access to its renowned collection and electronic resources. In addition to preserving the original character of the reading room, the library faced an increasing demand to upgrade its infrastructure to meet the needs of library users and staff for the 21st century. To meet this mission, a team of restoration architects from Davis Brody Bond adapted the room to maximize efficiency of library service while maintaining the historic and aesthetic integrity of the space.

The restoration of the Rose Reading Room, one of the largest uncolumned rooms in the nation, also marked the preservation of one of New York City's most beloved spaces. "When this library opened in 1911, it was acclaimed for its advanced technologies and methods," said Jean Bowen, director of the Center for Humanities at the facility. "The current renovation lets us carry forward our tradition of providing innovative new services, while maintaining the original operating framework that has worked so well for so long."

Functional improvements to the Rose Reading Room include expanded capacity, faster and more reliable book delivery, a self-service copy center, improved access for readers with disabilities, and a reorganized open-shelf reference collection. Technical improvements include new electronic resources, a multimedia viewing area, and improved general and task lighting.

To allow most user stations to access data and power for library equipment and personal laptops, 30 of the 42 original tables were carefully restored. The 22-foot-long library tables were modified to provide power and data at each reader station. This upgrade involved the design of custom-made electrical grommets and cover

plates, which were fitted flush into the tabletops. The table pedestals and the floor slab were cored to provide for power and data conduits, which connect a new distribution raceway below the tabletop to conduits and cable trays on the stack level below.

The designers integrated a new book delivery system into the existing stack structure to provide faster and more reliable delivery of books to readers. New service desks and enclosures were designed to match the Carrère & Hastings designs; the artisans who constructed these items used the same construction methods the early 20th-century workers had followed.

The restoration of the walls and ceiling was complicated by the size of the room—297 feet long by 78 feet wide by 55 feet high. To provide access to the surfaces to be restored, the workers constructed a 50-foot-high scaffold that occupied two-thirds of the room. The ceiling murals had suffered serious damage over the years, making it difficult for the artisans to discern the original character of the images. After a series of tests and mock-ups determined their design and colors, the replicated murals were painted on canvas and applied to the ceiling in two sections.

The existing mechanical systems in the room were modified to provide quieter and more even distribution of air and to improve the comfort level of the space. To upgrade the lighting system, the designers modified the original lamps to improve their efficiency and designed new fixtures to meet current lighting standards but echo the spirit of the originals by Carrère & Hastings. For the design of the new lighting, the designers sought to minimize the intrusiveness of any new illumination. The goal was for the lighting to enhance the spirit of the original Carrère & Hastings design yet meets the needs of library users today.

Working with the lighting design firm Fisher Marantz Stone, the architects sought to improve task lighting at reading tables as well as lighting for the bookcases under the balconies. The existing lighting at many of the reading tables was unevenly distributed and inadequate. The lamps, designed by Carrère & Hastings, were refurbished with higher-wattage bulbs, and the interiors of the shades were painted white to diffuse the light more evenly across the surface of the tables. For greater illumination throughout the reading room, the bulb wattage was increased in the ceiling chandeliers.

Opposite:
View of the room from the south wall

2

The original Carrère & Hastings design called for incandescent wall wash light fixtures to light the bookcases under the balconies. Over the years, these fixtures had been replaced with fluorescent strips. During the restoration, the designers uncovered the original drawings and several of the original fixtures. In reviewing these, they realized the Carrére & Hastings design had a reflector profile almost identical to that of modern wall wash fixtures made by Elliptar. They modified the standard profile of these fixtures with a bronze finish to create a more efficient design that imitated the shape of the Carrère & Hastings fixtures. These fixtures were then integrated into the design of the balcony edge; the resulting even illumination of the books turned this area into a focal feature of the reading room.

In addition to illuminating the bookcases, these fixtures light the tops of a nearby row of low shelves that serve as a reading surface.

Through a series of studies, Fisher Marantz Stone developed a lens assembly with a wide spread for the fixtures, which light the horizontal surface of the low bookcases without creating a visible source of glare. In the spirit of the room, this single fixture acts as both a wall wash and a task light, eliminating the clutter of additional fixtures.

A 2006 study funded by the Bill & Melinda Gates Foundation found that 99 percent of public library branches have Internet access. As technology takes on a greater role in our daily lives, it is important to incorporate this technology into the operations and services of our public libraries to meet the needs of the general public, library staff, and administration. For the Rose Reading Room of the New York Public Library, Davis Brody Bond designed an extensive restoration that seamlessly incorporates technology into the space with minimal impact on its historic aesthetic character.

2   Exterior view of the building
Opposite:
    Information desk

4

1	Vestibule	5	Public catalog room	9	Self-service copy
2	South hall	6	Reference desk	10	Book pick-up and return
3	North hall	7	A/V stations	11	Book delivery system from stacks
4	Staff enclosure	8	Supervised reading room	12	Copy services

5

6

7

8

9

4 Floor plan
5 New reading areas showing workstations
6 Shelf detail
7 View of the room looking north
8 Restored ceiling with new mural
9 Ceiling detail

10

10 Book return
11 Restored Caen stone walls and new lighting
Opposite:
    East-looking view of the entrance lobby
    showing newly designed lighting fixtures

11

Editing the Ordinary

CoOP Editorial, Santa Monica, California

Pugh + Scarpa Architecture

The remodel for the interior of this 1963 Frank Gehry-designed, single-story building offered Pugh + Scarpa the opportunity to expand on Gehry's early, energetic willingness to explore refined materials and plastic forms. The 47,000-square-foot Modernist box, an early commercial tenant building now occupied by CoOP Editorial, a video-editing facility, provided a clean, well-proportioned architectural shell for testing the craft qualities of new technologies.

The CoOP Editorial program called for three separate, soundproof video-editing bays where staff could spend long hours focused on editing screens, removed from the day-to-day business environment. Pugh + Scarpa established a design strategy to address the challenge of providing these spaces in a building not ideally suited for them: the design team would divide the program needs, placing the editing bays and individual office functions to one side of the building, while more active and public spaces would become floating elements. Conceptually, the conference room, executive producer's office, lounge areas, and restrooms became independent objects within the space. As is typical of Pugh + Scarpa's work, the program, material exploration, and individualistic expression of form became determinates for transcending traditional craft technologies and using new fabrication technologies to elevate ordinary materials in highly articulated sculpted forms. In other words, new technologies and technical fabrication processes enabled design innovation.

In early designs, the team introduced spatial flow by opening up floor-to-ceiling windows across the rear elevation, developing sight lines "from outside to the inside and to the outside again," as architect Scarpa describes it. Potential blocks to the open-transparency concept emerged in the requirement for three soundproof editing booths, as well as several administrative support offices, a conference room, the executive producer's office, and a lounge area. The architects' technically driven design solution reflected the programmed goals—accommodating the program's soundproof editing-booth requirements within the given width of the building, and retaining the existing metal obstructions along the front of Gehry's original façade—at the same time allowing for the illumination of natural light by way of newly created rear windows.

Pugh + Scarpa's concept had to acknowledge the important function of the editing booths as special enclaves for creativity that demanded long periods of concentrated work with dim lighting conditions. They sought to create a highly articulated wall that divided the shell from front to back, spanning the structure's 100-foot length. This datum spine allowed for the design team to separate the editing booths from public spaces, giving the program clarity and providing the opportunity for technical innovation.

The articulated wall was made possible through the use of digital modeling. Its waves, reflecting the poetics of ocean waves, were created with a series of 74 carved, glue-laminated panels. Digitally designed models were programmed to cut the panels with a computer numerically controlled rotator—a CNC machine. The panels formed a veneer system—a skin or surface wrapper—that was sculpted by direct automation, eliminating traditional handcrafted labor.

Digital modeling and the translation of image to reality with the technology of the CNC rotor made possible the transformation of lumber into sculpted form and space. The structural glue-lam lumber is now fluid wood, super-charged with energy and animation. The sculptured wall serves as a circulation spine through the office space, separating the concrete world of things from the creative world of story and fantasy in the editing booths.

The design team heightened the experience of tension among material, form, and experience by placing freestanding, colored, acrylic-paneled cubes in floating space, which contrast with the organic surfaced wall. To further test ideas of craft and construction traditions, layers of ⅛-inch colored acrylic sheets were assembled to build translucent walls for the conference room, executive office, and restrooms. These objects appear to float in space, as new skylights bathe each surface with natural light and backlight the walls to add depth and distance to the space. Light is used to order the space, while the rooms appear to be suspended above the floor because they sit on neoprene pads with deep reveals. The composition of light-transferring acrylic panels that appear as floating solids within the structured space, lighted by low-tech skylights, spotlights the technology of new materials in an innovative design solution.

Opposite:
Detail of the conference room

2

Transforming ordinary wood and acrylic into extraordinary spaces sets our senses "outside the frame," giving us a deeper understanding of object, material, and craft. As Larry Scarpa explains: "Art does not reproduce what we see; rather it makes us see." For Pugh + Scarpa, the desire for design innovation drives the exploration of materials and inquiry into the use of new technologies in a quest to edit the ordinary to "reveal the extraordinary."

2   Studio sitting area
3   Detail of CNC wood wall
4   Floor plan

3

1	Lobby	6	Vault	11	Avid room #2
2	Reception/island	7	Server room	12	Avid room #3
3	Kitchen area	8	Restroom	13	Avid room #4
4	Conference room	9	Rear lobby	14	Graphics area
5	Office	10	Avid room #1	15	Electrical
				16	Patio

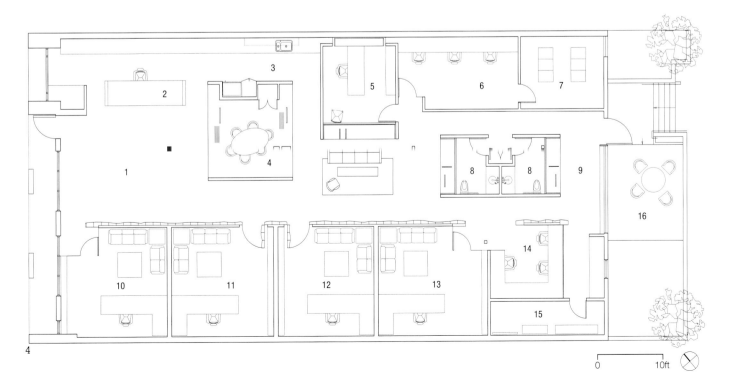

4

0   10ft

5 Overall view of studio sitting area looking west
6 Detail view of the sitting room area
7 Reception area and kitchen

5

6

Editing the Ordinary

7

In broad terms, process management refers to the establishment of a system, or process, to measure and control a project, job, or event. Architecture is often thought of as a profession driven by creative design—with the ultimate goal of conceiving of new or unique ways of designing buildings and structures. While it is true that design creativity is the most common means of measuring achievement in architecture in the minds of most, the less appreciated art of process management is critical to the success of every project.

The four projects included in this chapter vary greatly in size, scope, budget, and goals. They include a loft residence in the Tribeca neighborhood of New York City; the offices and production facilities for a Santa Monica film company; the relocation of an online student resources company to the Backslash building in Culver City; and the restoration of the neglected 1922 Detroit Opera House to its original splendor as a world-class building for the arts.

In spite of their differences, all four projects share a common success story as examples of exemplary process management. For the offices of XAP Corporation and the offices and production facilities of Reactor Films, the design firms were able to achieve the design goal while operating within an unusually tight schedule and budget. The Detroit Opera House restoration project required managing a large design and consulting team on a complex effort that also involved the work of artisans, skilled craft specialists, and an architectural conservation consultant. In renovating a loft space in an old garment factory building for the Gardner-James Residence, the design firm came upon an unusual situation—the previous tenant had been evicted and the process of removal and renovation was slower than expected. A conventional design would have necessitated a lengthy construction period, however, due to the delay, requirements of New York real estate law, and the needs of the client, the construction period was shortened to 30 days. To meet this unusual timeframe, the design firm had to find an entirely unique solution.

In the design of the Garner-James Residence in the Tribeca neighborhood of New York City by Valerio Dewalt Train Associates, meeting the unusually demanding 30-day construction schedule required new methods of coordination of the design and construction team. The process of closing on the space was put on hold by extenuating circumstances, preventing the developer from maintaining his published schedule. As time passed by and construction moved at a slow pace, the client finally demanded that construction be completed within 30 days of closing. All of the previous assumptions by the design team for the construction process had to be discarded, and a new strategy was unveiled. The design team would utilize the time available before construction commenced to complete the loft design and fabrication off site, and subsequently ship the entire new design to New York. The design concept took into account this new construction technique, and once fabrication was completed, the parts were assembled in a warehouse in Chicago, disassembled, loaded onto trucks, and driven to New York. The nearly 3,000 components were then lifted into the apartment by crane, and a crew of craftsmen and supervising personnel from the Chicago fabricators miraculously completed

construction within the 30 day period. The success of the project team in meeting their goal can be attributed to bringing ingenuity to their approach to process management.

In the case of Pugh + Scarpa's design for the XAP Corporation, the design firm had to deliver the completed project within a tight schedule. The designers relied on their experience with previous fast-track projects and utilized a collaborative effort with close coordination between the client, contractor, and architect to speed up the decision-making process. Pugh + Scarpa utilized innovative process management to complement design innovation by scheduling the design and fabrication of singular sculptural objects and large furniture pieces in a simultaneous fashion. The architect/developer's approval constraints and accelerated project schedule created the need for a highly structured approval process to solve program and design goals. The tight schedule dictated resolving design decisions with direct client and fabricator input. As a result of their willingness to collaborate and multi-task during the design process, the design firm was able to save the client money while delivering the project within the schedule.

Pugh + Scarpa utilized a slightly different approach in the design of the offices and production facilities for Reactor Films. In this instance, a 14-week schedule from preliminary design to move-in

required a programming strategy that structured tasks into distinct areas that could be developed and detailed in phases with quick approval by the client and dimensioned into construction. The production company Reactor Films was housed in an existing 1930's Art Deco structure in Santa Monica that would need to be renovated. Pugh + Scarpa used a charrette-style process management approach to meet this demanding timeline. Different programmed areas were subdivided to be studied and developed independently, progressing to greater levels of refinement and resolution as construction schedules demanded. This involved a complex set of relationships of time management, budget, design resolution, construction/fabrication, communication, and quality control expectations. The architect essentially worked with "one take" by placing ideas on 11-by 17-inch sheets of vellum in freehand pencil. Designs were then sent for client review and faxed to collaborators for input—creating a process similar to a charrette, and resulting in a design that evolved at full scale.

For the renovation of the renowned Detroit Opera House, architects Albert Kahn Associates, Inc engaged and coordinated an extensive archival and field research, programming, and design and construction process that took place over three years. The Opera House is a 2,700-seat theater auditorium in Detroit's "necklace" district, designed for stage productions and silent films. Coordinating programming and preliminary design activities with JPRA Architects accommodated modern opera performance and operations. This allowed integrating an originally isolated office block adjacent to the structure for the administration of theater productions and educational programs planned by the client. At the time of the purchase in 1989 by Michigan Opera Theatre, 90 percent of the plasterwork had deteriorated and was destroyed beyond salvaging. The design firm engaged in extensive archival research to ensure accuracy in reconstructing plaster motifs, moldings, and decorative elements. Albert Kahn Associates engaged in extensive coordination with multiple specialists to restore the Opera House back to its original splendor.

The projects that have achieved outstanding process management as identified in this chapter were each unique in project type and scope, and each required distinct design solutions to meet the original design goal. In each example, the design firm demonstrated a unique capability to adjust to difficult or unusual circumstances that required original thinking and familiarity with the tools, processes, and procedures necessary to manage complex projects.

Exceptional Process Management

Manageable Creativity

Gardner-James Residence, New York, New York

Valerio Dewalt Train Associates

"Necessity is the mother of invention." This old adage couldn't be more true than for the project that converted this amazing loft in the Tribeca neighborhood of New York City into a residence in just 30 days on site. The client had purchased a loft space in an old garment factory building not yet vacated by its commercial occupants. The slow process of eviction and renovation left the new owners in a real-estate bind. They had to build out and occupy the space within 30 days of their closing date. What kind of space can be built in only one month—in Manhattan? To answer this question, the architects devised a unique solution using equally unconventional means.

The design, for what might have been a perfectly ordinary loft, is allegorical. The architect likens the solution to an elaborate costume of galvanized metal in a theatrical production. The metal is "critical to the drama, contributing to the suspension of belief and covering the truth with a comfortable fiction." Yet, for all its remarkable allusion, the loft is simply a collection of metal objects, like appliances for living, manufactured elsewhere and delivered to the site to form an instant set for living.

To further the allusion, the architect explains that the functions for living are "hidden in the folds of the costume." In fact, deep pockets unfold to reveal a kitchen, sleeping platforms, places to study, and an entertainment alcove. The resulting sets are compelling and remarkably comfortable for living. The story of the creation of the loft reveals the exemplary process management the architecture firm put in place to accomplish this project despite its limiting situation. The architects' own description outlines their way of solving the problem:

"In the few months right after our client purchased the apartment, we began working on a [conventional] design that would have required a lengthy construction phase after our client closed on the apartment—the closing according to New York real estate law had to wait until the [developer's portion of the] construction work was completed. This meant the client had to wait for the leases to expire, then they would have to wait for the developer to complete its work, and finally they would have to wait for us to complete the build-out.

We soon learned the developer was [unable] to keep to his published schedule. The existing tenants were not leaving the building, and the construction work they were able to start was moving at a snail's pace. Finally one Friday afternoon, I got a call from our exasperated client—he wanted our construction phase shortened … to 30 days.

[We had] to completely change the ground rules. Obviously, I had plenty of time before we could start work in the apartment, but only a very short time to complete the work once it began. The answer seemed both simple and obvious: take advantage of the slow pace of the developer to complete the design and fabrication of the apartment [off site] and then ship everything to New York."

The architect's concept for the loft as an allusion to the elements of a costume worked to define the space, but it made the apartment shell somewhat like a gallery—a blank space in which to complete an art installation. The art would transform the empty box into a completed apartment—in record time.

The design concept treated the interior as an empty box in which to insert a series of metal objects. These objects would house particular functions, such as the kitchen and the home office. The objects would also divide the space, creating semi-enclosed areas for living, dining, and guest accommodations (privacy would be provided by floor-to-ceiling curtains). Once the design was set, the designers developed the objects in three dimensions, using a standard CAD program. The interiors of each object were developed as millwork, using mostly birch veneer. Surrounding and attached to the millwork would be a skin of galvanized sheet metal. Full-size patterns were developed for the sheet metal, including the hidden fastening system to join the parts together.

Once the fabrication was complete, the parts were assembled in a warehouse in Chicago, then disassembled, loaded onto trucks, and driven to New York. In two hours, the nearly 3,000 components were lifted by crane into the apartment through one of the large windows. Work began with a crew of New York artisans and supervising personnel from the Chicago fabricators in a stripped-down space with white drywall enclosures and a mahogany floor. Construction was completed in 30 days.

Ingenuity, in process as well as design, created an extraordinary space for living.

Opposite:
Overall view of dining/living space from the front door

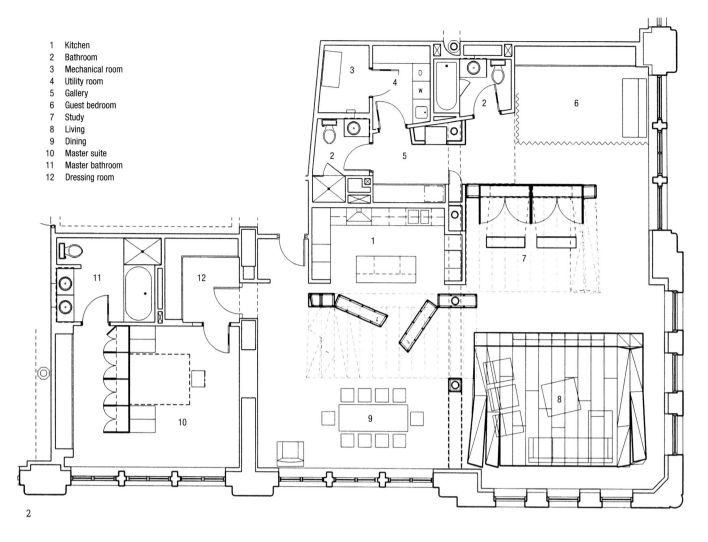

1   Kitchen
2   Bathroom
3   Mechanical room
4   Utility room
5   Gallery
6   Guest bedroom
7   Study
8   Living
9   Dining
10 Master suite
11 Master bathroom
12 Dressing room

2

3

2 Floor plan
3 Living platform, looking past column to kitchen area
4 View from living platform to dining space

4

5 View of dining area through to kitchen, doors closed
6 Edge of living platform, kitchen and office doors in the background
7 Living platform looking to partially open door of kitchen
Opposite:
    View from dining area to kitchen, doors open

5

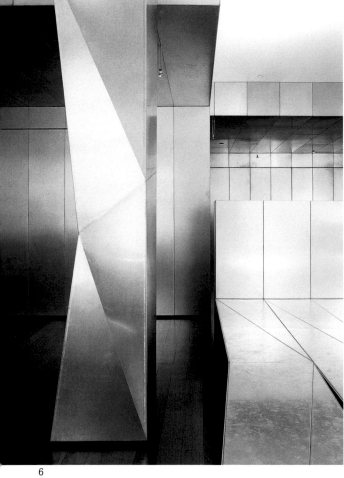

6

7

9

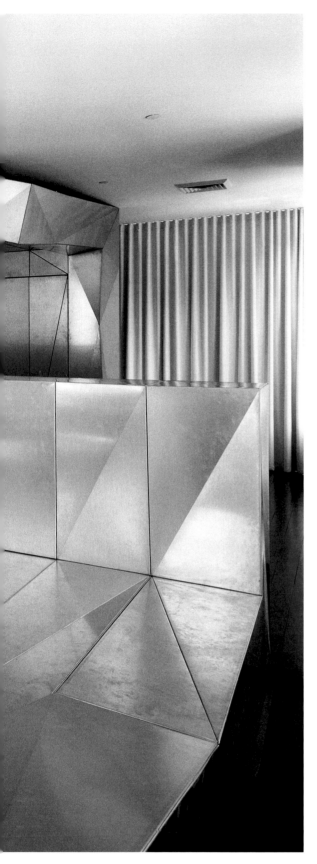

10

11

9   View of living platform, kitchen in left background,
     office in right background, doors closed
10 Doors of living platform, concealing electronics
11 Living platform

12

13

15

12 Master bedroom
13 Closets/dressing room, looking out to the street
14 Office, doors open
15 View from office through to the living platform and dining area

14

Beauty in Form and Material
XAP Corporation, Culver City, California

Pugh + Scarpa Architecture

As a small start-up firm, XAP Corporation required a large image. The online management resource service for students applying for higher education opportunities, with a staff of 55 young professionals, chose to relocate to a 20,000-square-foot space in the Backslash building designed by Eric Owen Moss in Culver City, California. To prepare for its move, the company commissioned Pugh + Scarpa Architecture to design the interior of its new offices. This small but expanding company realized the value of creating an open, aesthetically flowing environment that would appeal to the youthful sensibilities of both its young employees and college-bound clients.

The owner/developer of the Moss-designed Backslash building put significant constraints on Pugh + Scarpa's work: new tenant design improvements that significantly touch or infringe on the structure were forbidden, and all phases of the design had to be submitted to the building architect for review and approval. In addition to these limits, XAP needed the project completed in just four months and within a budget of $1,020,000.

Pugh + Scarpa had experience with fast-tracked projects, and its ability to deliver a completed project in a short time came from its systematic method of working with client, contractor, and architect to collaborate in a rapid decision-making mode. This was facilitated by the fact that the architects' drawings functioned as both presentation and construction documents, which supported the collaborative process and the need for a quick turnaround when decisions had to be made.

Pugh + Scarpa viewed the architect/developer's approval constraints and the client's accelerated project schedule as issues that increased the design challenge and created the need for a highly structured approval process to solve program and design goals. Rather than waiting for top-down approvals, the team members engaged in integrated thinking that anticipated decisions. Fast-paced scheduling dictated that design decisions would be resolved with direct client and fabricator input. Innovative process management complemented design innovation by scheduling the design and fabrication of sculptural objects and large furniture pieces simultaneously. Close coordination and drawing documentation tracked design development with permit registration, fabrication, and on-site installation.

Beginning with the programmatic requirements, the architects zoned dense areas of like functions together so that design resolution and fabrication could be carried out in phases. This method isolated areas that had yet to be completely designed or contracted for production from those ready for construction. Some employees could address the needs of one component of the fabrications, while others were developing and designing other components. As an example, the construction path for building and fabricating offices and workstations was kept separate from the work needed to design and build public areas containing the board and conference rooms.

As one of the design goals, XAP Corporation wanted to provide working environments that projected a strong visual image—for clients as well as employees—of a successful, leading-edge technology company that provides up-to-date online information services for higher education. Its design innovation had to equal and maintain the freshness and innovation of the Internet. The Pugh + Scarpa design houses offices and workstations in dense areas of similar size and shape set in the open landscape of the building shell, purposefully juxtaposing them against the freer, more open public areas. The regimented organization of the work areas forms a backdrop for the more dynamic and fluid design of the meeting room enclosures. These creative sculptural forms are accented with well-crafted, innovative furniture pieces.

Visitors entering the office must travel 30 feet from the entry to reach the reception counter, giving them an opportunity to experience the dynamic composition of the public area. The composition reveals the interplaying relationships of the organic boardroom and conference room forms and their interior spaces as contrasted with the suspended horizontal surfaces of the reception counter. The two sculptural meeting rooms give XAP Corporation an immediate identity, while serving their functions. Although these two imposing forms appear to be wrapped in soft, textured material, upon closer examination their surfaces are seen to be the back side of the interior walls' plaster surfaces—soft plaster pushed through perforated metal lath. While the exterior of the meeting rooms are heavily textured, the interior surfaces are smooth and molded to a creamy plasticity. This duality repeats throughout the XAP Corporation design.

1 Sections
2 View of conference room

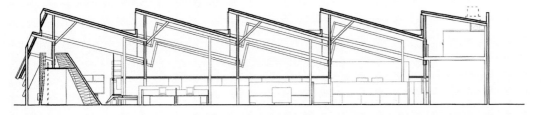

SECTION A

SECTION B

0   15ft

1

2

3

4

5

6

7

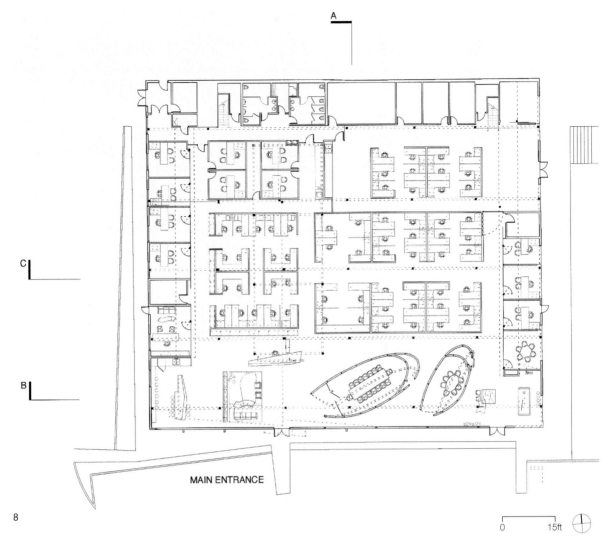

A

C

B

MAIN ENTRANCE

8

0   15ft

3&4   Rear view of conference room
   5   Lounge area and ventilation outlets
   6   Reception desk
   7   Interior detail
   8   Floor plan
   9   Exploded axonometric of a conference room

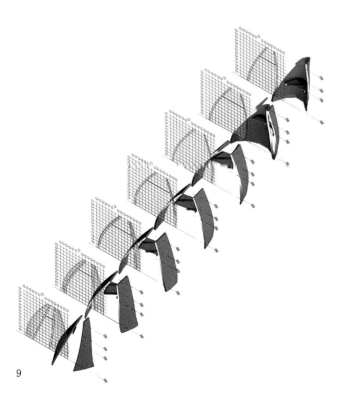

9

The practice of taking ordinary building materials and standard construction methods and finishing them to a level of refinement and clarity characterizes much of Pugh + Scarpa's work. The XAP Corporation offices demonstrate the possibilities for engaging in a formal exploration of materials within an accelerated timetable, and the approval constraint and four-month design-build schedule forced the design to evolve quickly. Computer models and digital communication allowed the design team to make decisions and stay one step ahead of manufacturers and fabricators, often using rough rendered models as fabrication documents. When using an accelerated design and production process, it is easy to abbreviate the exploration of detail, material, and form. Pugh + Scarpa, however, considers this exploration an important part of the dynamic process of building construction: composing a building is like composing a work of art—changes and corrections are made to achieve the desired effect. The XAP office design demonstrates layers of spatial content, richness of detail, successful user interface, and ultimately user satisfaction.

A Film Firm in a Can

Reactor Films, Santa Monica, California

Pugh + Scarpa Architecture

An existing 1930's Art Deco tile-faced structure in Santa Monica became the perfect setting for Reactor Film's newly renovated offices and production facilities. Within the tight project schedule, Pugh + Scarpa provided a dramatic design for the Santa Monica production company, which specializes in commercials and music videos. The 14-week schedule, from preliminary design to move-in, required fresh thinking for the architect and client and inspired Pugh + Scarpa's dynamic reuse of a ubiquitous Southern California icon— the shipping container. Strong visual imagery was created by using familiar materials in unfamiliar ways, creating a stage set in space, which was executed using a fast-track design-build process.

The 14-week timetable necessitated a programming strategy for structuring tasks into distinct areas that could be developed and detailed in phases, quickly approved by the client, and dimensioned for construction. Design decisions and detailing had to be accomplished in close collaboration with contractor, client, and fabricator. The contractor and fabricator worked closely with the architect to ensure expert direction and expedite decision-making and budget allowances. Because of the architect's past experience with similar accelerated projects, the rigorous technical aspects and program requirements were solved first. Different programmed areas were subdivided for independent study and development, progressing to greater levels of refinement and resolution as the construction schedule demanded. This method resulted in a complex set of relationships between time management, budget, design resolution, construction/fabrication, communication, and quality control expectations.

During the first week of design, construction began. Permits were issued in the second week. The architect created a fast and flexible format by placing ideas on 11- by 17-inch sheets of vellum in freehand pencil. These drawings were first drawn as presentation images for client review and then faxed to collaborators for expert input and modification as required. The immediacy of working with "one take," as Pugh + Scarpa describes it, increased the design's spontaneity. And as in a charrette, according to partner Gwynne Pugh, "contrary to expectations, the time constraint didn't compromise design; if anything, it actually catalyzed the work." This resulted in a design that evolved at full scale.

The renovation of the client's small masonry structure, the modest budget, and super-accelerated occupation schedule permitted the architects to respond directly and intuitively to the interior renovation problem. The open street context required a direct flow program, and combined with the client's particular machine interest, unleashed a creative industrial vernacular vocabulary for the project. The building's open Art Deco façade and the desire of the client to have an "industrial-looking interior," opened possibilities for a familiar Southern California industrial salvage aesthetic—the corrugated shipping container.

The industrial shipping crate, now modified for programmed use and placed to be clearly visible from the street, introduces a "designed" tension between the old, comfortable façade that frames the steel icon—the refined shipping crate. Set within a white interior space of light and supported by other well-composed and beautiful industrial classic furniture pieces, the salvaged corrugated shipping container is now an object in space set on center stage. Programmed as the conference room, the container serves as the gravitational focus of the facility. This resurrected urban artifact both structures the focus and layers the experiences that visually and programmatically weave through Pugh + Scarpa's solution.

The container as conference room has been altered to meet program needs and further the exploration of the firm's ordinary materials quest. Shortened and made wider, wrapped in treated steel and perforated metal screens, contrast is provided by interventions of fine wood panels and smooth concrete surfaces. The conference box sits atop structural concrete piers accessed by a bold cantilevered sculptured concrete stair. The whole composition is set in opposition to a custom-designed steel-and-wood reception desk. A further understanding of the architect's intentions to realize light and materials as ordering devices, as well as focusing elements, is structuring movement with strategic placement of overhead luminous slots and constructing semi-translucent partition walls for production staff offices. Light, material, and compositional perfection establish frame and pattern, engaging the occupants as cinematic actors within the architectural space.

1

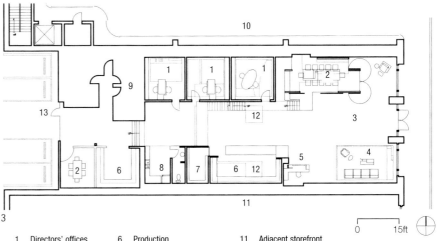

3

1 Directors' offices
2 Conference room
3 Lobby
4 Waiting area
5 Reception
6 Production
7 Storage/computer/data
8 Kitchen
9 Staff offices
10 Public parking structure
11 Adjacent storefront
12 Skylights above
13 Service/staff entry

2

4

5

1 View of conference room
2 Detail view of stairs and conference room
3 Floor plan
4 View from back toward Fourth Street entry
5 View of bridge toward back

Spotlight on Center Stage
Detroit Opera House, Detroit, Michigan

Albert Kahn Associates, Inc.

Bright lights, big city, lavish colors, and flamboyant fans. Three years of extensive renovation and restoration returned the long-neglected historic Detroit Opera House in Detroit's Necklace District to its full grandeur. Designed in 1922 by Detroit architect C. Howard Crane for stage productions and silent films, the once-opulent 2,700-seat theater auditorium had fallen into decades-long ruin and neglect, including substantial water damage to its beautiful decorative plaster motifs from a long-standing leaky roof. The architecture firm Albert Kahn Associates, Inc. resurrected the building to serve as a world-class venue for operatic and dance productions for the revived Michigan Opera Theatre Company. The restoration of the building has in turn helped revitalize the surrounding area in downtown Detroit.

Albert Kahn Associates, Inc. oversaw the complex restoration project, which required management of several different consulting firms, independent craftspeople and artisans, and the renovation of the 24,000-square-foot theater complex and 75,000-square-foot administrative tower next door. Using consultants, artisans, and skilled craft specialists, the design team directed and coordinated archival and field research, programming, design, and construction phases over three years. Programming and preliminary design activities were coordinated with JPRA Architects, architects for the stage house and administrative tower addition. This was necessary to accommodate the needs of contemporary theater productions, restore historical details, and program the addition to the original 1922 stage house. An expanded orchestra pit was incorporated to allow for larger ensembles, and the architects improved circulation and accessibility in creative ways by enlarging restrooms for convenience and comfort and updating exits to meet requirements. The office block adjacent to the theater was incorporated into the project to house the administrative aspect of theater productions and spaces for educational programs.

When the Michigan Opera Theatre purchased the opera house in 1989, 90 percent of the plasterwork had deteriorated beyond salvaging. Albert Kahn Associates conducted extensive archival research to ensure accuracy in reconstructing plaster motifs, moldings, and decorative elements. Molds for plaster ceiling modules were constructed on site, where artisans completed the molding process for skilled workers to fit into the original ceiling patterns.

The architects commissioned architectural conservation consultant Steve Seebolm to determine the historic colors of the original theater. Despite the deteriorated interior plaster and water-damaged surfaces, forensic analysis of more than 750 surface samples established the original color palette of the theater. Aided by a binocular microscope and a supporting 7,000-K light source, Seebolm revealed the original deep regal blue, gold, and natural ochre paints of the public spaces. To establish and maintain an antique look, a tinted glaze was recommended with the application of the new color palette.

The Detroit Opera House was originally designed to recall the opulent decoration and eclectic styles of the grand European opera house traditions popular in the 18th and 19th centuries. Because the site required a side entry, the designers had to forgo the traditional European grand entry. However, one of the street entry lobbies transitions to a restored vaulted arcade lined with Tiffany-style overhead glass panels, bathing the space in subtle, soft blue light, which leads to the grand foyer.

These two opposing street entry lobbies meet in the grand foyer, a three-story vertical space dressed in gilded details and reliefs. The balustrades on the stairs mimic the flamboyant style to every detail. Reproducing the original carpet pattern was a challenge as only a small remnant remained. Three massive brass and crystal chandeliers, restored to original detail, light the whole ensemble.

Past the grand foyer, the theater auditorium unfolds to reveal a masterful architectural performance of color, plaster detail, and gracious space. The proscenium arch and central oculus dominate the auditorium. The oculus was completely rebuilt from photographs and constructed in plaster to match the original. The eye glides from it to the stage, which is trimmed in gilded ochres, deep browns, and rich regal blues that were painstakingly matched. Giant plaster reliefs of the ceiling provide a perfect frame for the stage and proscenium dressed in the replicated curtain. Seventeen private boxes, also replicated from old photographs, make up the grand-tier level. Their upholstered chairs and bright red carpet repeat the original elegance of this area of the theater.

Opposite:
Detail view of restored arcade

2

The renovation and restoration of the historic Detroit Opera House by Albert Kahn Associates required bringing together and coordinating multiple specialists. Extensive archival research and on-site investigation required the efforts of expert consultants and craftspeople. Along with their work, engineers, contractors, and programmers were needed to successfully restore and renovate the 1922 structure to its original splendor. The complexity of this project to revitalize a historic structure to serve as a modern operatic and dance theater exhibits the importance of creative process management as well as creative design solutions.

2   Exterior setting
Opposite:
    New stage house addition

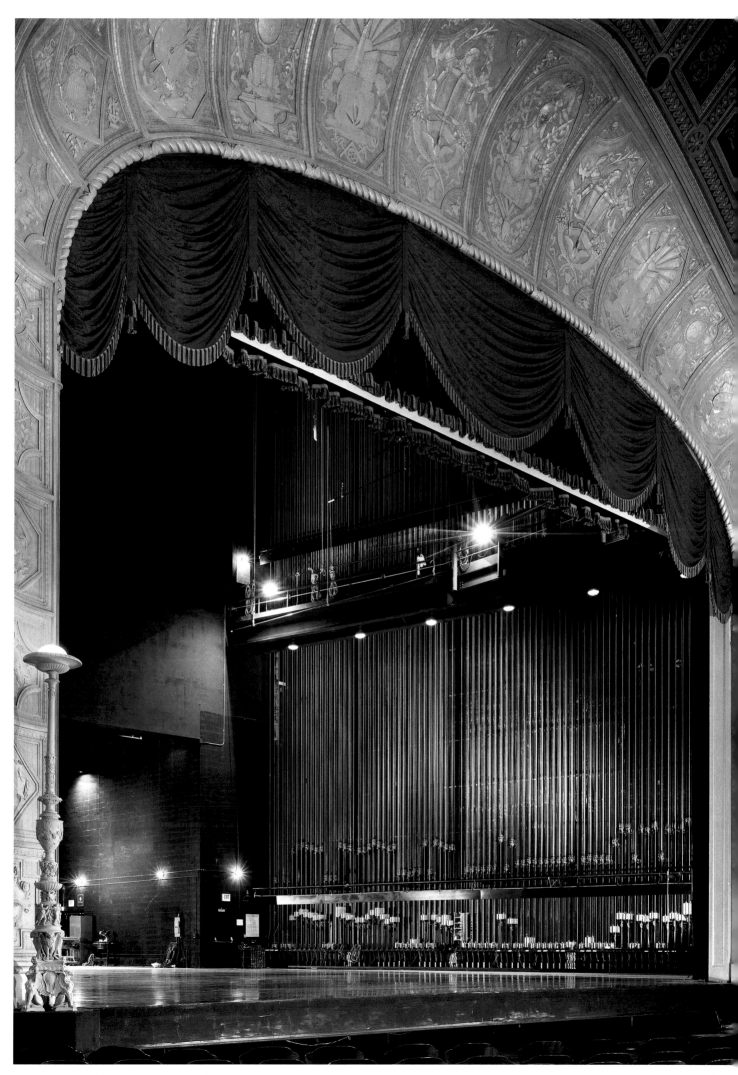

4

4   Preserved historical conditions in the administrative wing
5   View of preserved original ceiling and ripple art glass salvaged from the on-site demolition
6   Ground floor plan
7   Fifth floor plan

5

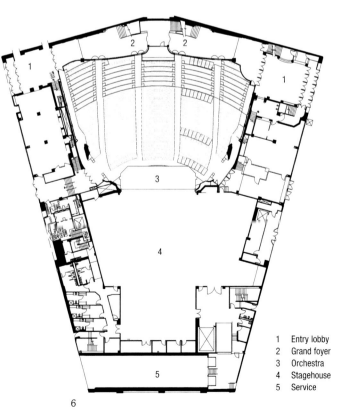

6

1   Entry lobby
2   Grand foyer
3   Orchestra
4   Stagehouse
5   Service

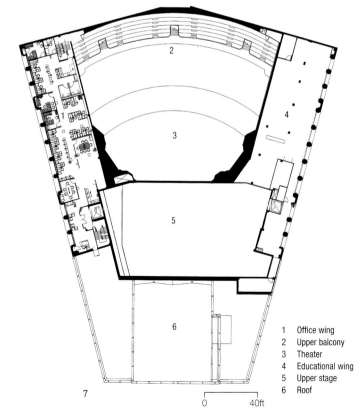

7

1   Office wing
2   Upper balcony
3   Theater
4   Educational wing
5   Upper stage
6   Roof

0   40ft

9

10

11

Opposite:
Grand Foyer
9   View from the balcony
10 Detail of staircase
11 Restored theater vault

12

13

12 View of private boxes and restored ceilings
13 View of the three-story Grand Foyer

The four projects in this section demonstrate a commitment to social progress and environmentally sensitive design and conservation. Their designs create environments that affect the way people live, learn, and worship. Ranging from a Roman Catholic church in Louisiana to a mixed-use, high-rise complex in China, these buildings offer their users and visitors a place for interaction with others, for solitude, and for mental growth.

The goal of improving the social/environmental aspect of architectural projects—defined broadly as "innovations to benefit and improve the quality of life in the present and future"—has seen significant growth and acceptance in the mainstream. In the projects featured here, the use of daylighting, natural materials, and innovations in technology reflects an interest in the environmental aspects of these projects. The social features of each project are supported by its relationship with its community and society, whether it is a college campus, an urban neighborhood, or a high-density setting.

At the turn of the 20th century, concern for the environment and how it relates to the human components of interior space became an increasingly important aspect of design. Each of the projects selected for this filter responds to these concerns in unique ways, particularly in how the designs respond to quality-of-life issues and how they address the social/environmental relationship.

The design intent for Saint Jean Vianney Catholic Church in Baton Rouge, Louisiana, designed by Trahan Architects, is rooted in the Vatican II liturgy. The design for the new sanctuary focused on providing a gathering space that celebrates the value of Christian assembly. Natural light and panoramic views activate the worship space and encourage a communal feeling devoid of boundaries. The idea that each person shares an equal place at the table was the inspiration for the appearance of the communal room, or sanctuary. The designers derived from this concept the sense of volume, spatial organization, sequence, light quality, material selection, and detail in their design solution.

Smith-Buonanno Hall in Providence, Rhode Island, was built in 1907 as a two-story gymnasium for Pembroke College, which later merged with Brown University. The building was in its original condition when the client commissioned William Kite Architecture to transform it into something the university could use today. The architects created a classroom facility/lecture hall that works well in the campus environment at Brown. They met the challenge of doing new work within the fabric of an old building while paying homage to what has come before. The result is a "new" building that is striking in its inventiveness.

In a similar vein, Weiss-Manfredi took an unused gymnasium and converted it into a library, providing something desperately needed in the New York City community of Queens. The Robin Hood Foundation/NYC Public Library proves that design can transform a community in need. To convert an institutional building into a beloved library, the architect used well-thought-out elements to devise an affordable-yet-fun project. Both Smith-Buonanno Hall and the Robin Hood Foundation/NYC Public School Library exemplify successful adaptive reuse.

A project that expresses the personality of a particular community is the Jin Mao Tower in Shanghai, China, designed by Skidmore, Owings & Merrill. The building's pagoda-style form and the use of the number eight—considered a lucky number by the Chinese—in the tower's setbacks integrates references to regional history and culture with high-level current technologies. Since 2001, a skyscraper boom has focused on creating bigger and better structures. In the context of these huge man-made spaces, the building itself provides an environment for social interactions. For the interiors, the client wanted to establish a sense of harmony and unity between the building's architecture and its site and to create a sense of equilibrium for the complex and vast public spaces, which include retail stores, a lobby, and an observatory.

Each of these projects advances social and environmental goals in ways that are similar, yet markedly different. No matter where a building is located—from a church in harmony with nature to an urban high-rise in a high-density city—its environment affects its users. We must learn how to react to these environments. These projects have responded to this challenge; they are models of how we can improve our present and future quality of life.

Social Responsiveness

Spirit of Place

Trahan Architects

St. Jean Vianney Catholic Church in Baton Rouge embodies some of Trahan Architects' core architectural objectives: to explore and invent a new and more inclusive sense of community and to celebrate humanity's relationship with nature. Supported by this approach to the project and a commitment to the use of natural materials and light, the architects pursued the most fundamental intention of their design work—to illuminate and enrich a building's true purpose. As a result, they created a unique relationship between the church and its congregation that yielded a spirit of place.

The interiors of St. Jean Vianney are distinctive in two principal ways. First, the architectural identity was conceived from the inside out. Overall organizational, spatial, and material quality is driven by the spiritual and poetic themes of the intended interior experience. Second, the design of the interior creates a total environment, every feature and element of which sustains its organizing themes. The characteristic experience someone has in this type of space, where the purpose permeates every design component and every encounter, is one of immersion.

The belief that each has an equal place at the table generated the primary reference for the communal room, or sanctuary. The volume, spatial organization, sequence, light quality, material selection, and detail developed in the design all stem from this concept. The exterior massing of the building has a direct, formal relationship with the design of the interior. Taking this approach a step further, the muted, ornament-free identity of the exterior emphasizes the importance of the interior to the congregation.

Beyond basic architectural strategies, the architects maintained consistency of design throughout the interior environment by giving equal attention to the details of furniture and artifacts. They cultivated this concept by working collaboratively with artisans and contractors to design and tailor all building elements to serve the fundamental purpose of the building. The architects employed the simple use of forms and materials, and the play of natural light, to express spiritual intensity. Responding to a client request for minimal ornamentation, the architects created a space that focuses on the essentials of volume and mass.

The design is meant to challenge and comfort those who enter, reminding them of the mystery of faith while simultaneously enveloping them in an environment of natural beauty. A visitor passing through the narthex enters a luminous octagon of glass oriented to the cardinal directions and punctuated at the four compass points by triangular chapels. Entry to the octagon is situated along its north edge. Natural light and panoramic views of the natural setting invigorate the worship space and encourage a communal relationship devoid of boundaries.

The color of the interior of the church is neutral, allowing the people in attendance and the seasonal changes visible through the windows to add detail and richness to the space. As a result, the building is experienced differently when it is empty versus when people are present in celebration, creating a special bond between the church and its congregation.

This project design allows nature to penetrate interior spaces and creates authentic intimacy for worship. Because of the relationship it forges between the church building, nature, and the congregation, the design succeeds on both a social and an environmental level.

Opposite:
View through a portal toward the raised altar platform

2   Building section
3   Exterior view
4   Light emanating from within delineates the massing and materials
5   View of the congregation at morning mass

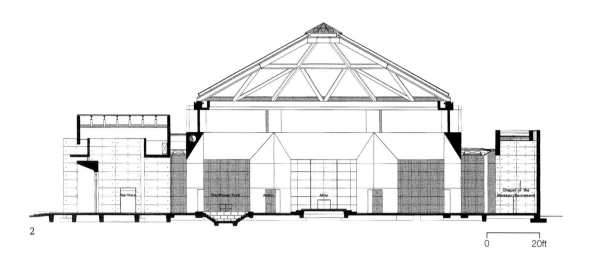

2

0   20ft

3

4

5

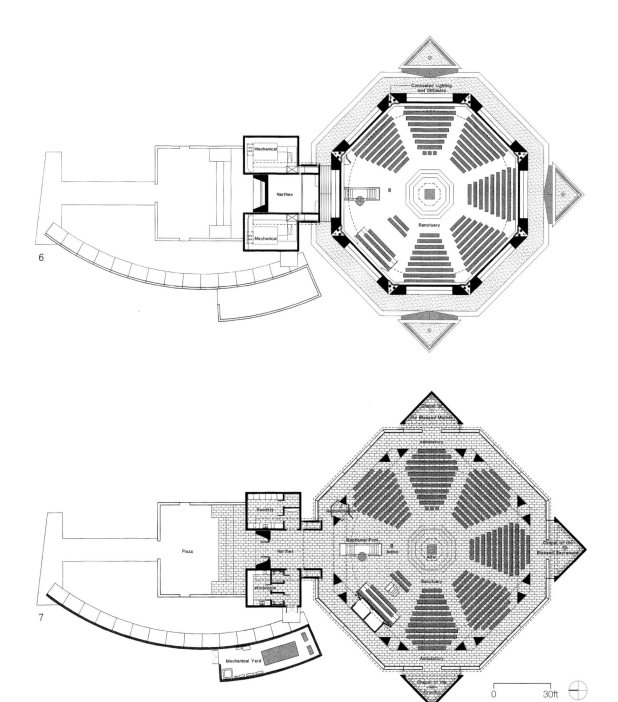

Concealed Lighting and Diffusers

Narthex

Sanctuary

Mechanical

Mechanical

6

Chapel of the Blessed Mother

Ambulatory

Sacristy

Reconciliation

Plaza

Narthex

Baptismal Font

Ambo

Altar

Chapel of the Blessed Sacrament

Workroom

Sanctuary

Mechanical Yard

Ambulatory

Chapel of the Crucifix

0   30ft

7

6   Upper floor plan
7   Lower floor plan
8   Solid concrete masses create a canvas for
    filtered light
9   Light pierces through the walls of windows,
    activating and engaging the space
10 Sunlight activates the Chapel of the
    Blessed Mother
11 Looking past the altar to the Chapel of the
    Blessed Mother

8

9

10

11

12

14

13

12   View of the entry portal's 14-foot bronze doors
13   Transition from entry to narthex to main body of church
14   View from the baptismal font to the ambo, the altar, and the tabernacle in the Chapel of the Blessed

15

15 View of the vaulted narthex
16 Looking through to the Chapel of the Blessed Mother
Opposite:
     The Reconciliation Chapel and the Holy Oils

16

18

18 The Holy Oil vessels are illuminated by fiber optics
    embedded in the concrete shelves
19 Simplicity of form expresses the significance of the Eucharist

19

Intelligent Design

William Kite Architects Inc.

Is this building the product of environmental adaptation or evolution, or the intentional design of a talented architect? The Smith-Buonanno Hall project stretches the boundaries of pure historic renovation, exceeds the expectations of adaptive reuse, and leads to a new standard for interior classroom space. The design intent was to create a definite shift in how we perceive space and how institutions can enhance learning. Through thoughtful renovation, an endangered structure evolved into an energy-efficient, functional, and accessible building. The designers' intent was to improve rather than replicate, to advance rather than imitate. The finished space is used for its intended purpose—as a classroom facility; more importantly, however, it inspires study and collegial collaboration. This project advances social and environmental goals by taking what was good from the old to construct a new, student-centered pedagogical environment.

Originally built in 1907 as Sayles Gymnasium, Smith-Buonanno Hall was designed by Stone, Carpenter and Willson in a Gothic style reminiscent of universities in Britain. Willson, a protégé of McKim, Mead and White, created this distinguished structure in the image of the former Pembroke campus, now a part of Brown University. A noteworthy original building, it was a significant piece of the history of both institutions. Vincent J. Buonanno said, "It bespeaks the Anglophilic leanings of Brown's patrons and leaders of a century ago and their understandable affection for some of the ancient English university campuses."

The project began as a restoration and in part as an adaptive reuse of the building. The exterior was meticulously restored reusing as much of the existing material as possible. Enough roof slates were salvaged to allow reuse on one whole side of the building, avoiding replacement of the entire roof with new material. New insulated-glass wood window sash was installed within the existing frames throughout the building to provide for a more energy-efficient exterior enclosure. Building entrances were redesigned to become fully accessible without the addition of exterior ramps or other obvious physical changes.

For the interior, the designers sought to maintain the atmosphere and quality of the original interior space, albeit for a completely new use. To this end, they studied new design elements that would contribute to and expand on the character of the building as conceived by the original architects. The prominent interior building space, with its distinctive wood trusses, brick walls, and wood floor, was respected in the new design. The existing woodwork, which on the surface appeared to be in poor condition, was found—after careful examination and the removal of layers of paint—to be quite sound.

The most difficult task for the architect of the renovation was dealing with the client's desire to create as many spaces as possible, while retaining a sense of openness and historical connection to the original architecture. The university wanted to insert a new floor level in the large gymnasium to introduce additional program space. The architects believed that the quality of the space in an open arrangement would be more valuable to the university than the extra floor area gained by constructing a new level. The design team convinced the university to proceed with their proposed design through a rigorous presentation of how an open plan could meet the university's programmatic needs. Once construction began and the administration could fully understand the design, university representatives became enthusiastic and excited by the design potential of the new spaces.

Within the two-story gym space, the designers placed new upper-story teaching spaces free of the exterior walls and ceiling. Supported by independent structures, the new spaces are designed to reveal the building's original structure. The original wood trusses still appear intact in the interior space of the lecture hall and common room, and the new enclosures frame areas of the exposed trusses in scale with the new classrooms and seminar rooms. Glazed ceiling and wall panels help contain the new teaching spaces and provide acoustical privacy while allowing a transparent view into and through the building. The character of the original space remains intact and obvious from many vantage points and at different floor levels.

New visual relationships showcase the architectural components of the original space. Photographic wall murals, reproduced from historic prints, located throughout the building, illustrate what the space looked like in the early 1900s. The bridge, balconies, and canopy over the audiovisual control room reflect the original mezzanine catwalk that encircled the building's interior perimeter. For a touch of nostalgia, the foul lines of the original basketball court remain on the new floor of the two-story common room.

1 Fixed seat classroom
2 Lecture hall

3

The design team made no attempt to replicate existing construction details. They intended to clearly contrast new and existing construction, allowing new and old to gracefully complement each other within the new environment. New construction details respect those of the original structure while expressing modernity in the use of materials, light, and color. New mechanical systems were integrated into the design and became visual elements, clearly expressing their purpose while providing energy-efficient heating and cooling to the new space. All lighting, light-control devices, sound systems, equipment, and computer-assisted teaching stations are fully integrated, state-of-the-art systems.

The renovated building has met with great favor among students, faculty, and the public. The most popular teaching space on campus, it is a highly sought-after venue for classes, meetings, and presentations. Shoggy Thierry Waryn of the Department of French Studies at Brown reports that "the success of the building among faculty is such that at the beginning of the semester, we all pray to have our classroom assignments in that building." Senior lecturer

Tori Smith reports: "I love the aerie that is Room 206, suspended over the old gymnasium floor, and I request it every semester for my Spanish language classes. The light pours in and we can look out into the trees and sky. My students love the space-age feel of the electronic controls, especially when they are activated by the professor in the room below ours and the blinds start to go down for what appears to us like no particular reason. We just laugh and pretend that we're being readied for blast-off!"

The project has also set a new standard for interior classroom space at the university, becoming "the benchmark for excellence in all subsequent capital projects," according to James Sisson, the university's construction manager.

Although the building has every modern convenience and technical capability, this cherished piece of Brown and Pembroke history has been respectfully preserved for future generations of students and faculty, who will continue to appreciate it. Students can learn from the past while developing their future.

3 Common area
4 Transverse section through new stairway
5 Accessible south entrance
6 Second floor hall at entrance stairway

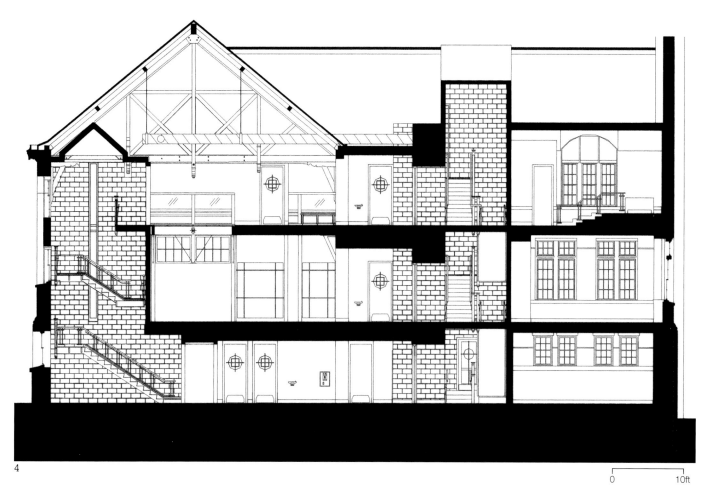

4

0   10ft

5

6

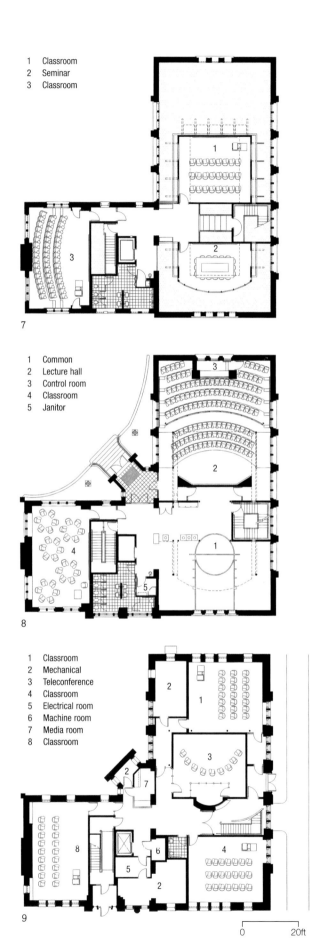

1 Classroom
2 Seminar
3 Classroom

7

1 Common
2 Lecture hall
3 Control room
4 Classroom
5 Janitor

8

1 Classroom
2 Mechanical
3 Teleconference
4 Classroom
5 Electrical room
6 Machine room
7 Media room
8 Classroom

9

0   20ft

10

11

7   Second floor plan
8   First floor plan
9   Ground floor plan
10   Projection booth at lecture hall
11   Lecture hall

12 Common area
13 Second floor seminar room
14 Second floor classroom
15 Longitudinal section through second floor classrooms

13

12

14

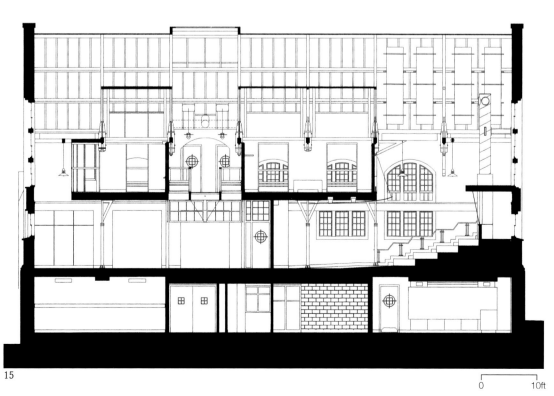

15

For the Life of a Bookworm

Robin Hood Foundation/Public School 42 Library, Queens, New York

Weiss/Manfredi

Architecture is at its best when it means something special to each user. Architects are at their best when their spaces inspire and engage us to seek new possibilities, challenge our conventions, and fulfill our dreams. Architecture also functions as a social art when it instills community pride and provides a *place* that can draw a community together.

Architects Weiss/Manfredi, working on a pilot project for New York City's Queens public schools, challenged conventional notions of the stuffy, serious school library by providing a place for fantasy, adventure, and the *bookworm* student. With pro bono architectural services and project funding from the Robin Hood Foundation, the architects' design for the library at NYC Public School 42 brings interior architecture and social art together for elementary school children in urban Queens. The library is an inspiring place for fun and learning in a community setting.

A place for gathering to engage in varied activities, this space transforms the idea of a conventional children's library into a magical place of possibilities. Inventiveness and creativity provide an interior landscape where young readers can discover the life of books: books as art and books as a part daily life. This singular library space also provides a medium for bringing people together and encouraging social interaction.

The library was relocated from a somewhat remote fourth-floor room in the school to a former gym on the first floor next to the entrance and cafeteria. The isolated fourth-floor location had limited student access and discouraged community use. The first-floor location generated greater street visibility and access, redefining the library's purpose and social placement within the school and the community.

The figural notion of a *bookworm* is a theme carried into the functional design of the library space via a well-crafted curvilinear book-wall that runs laterally through the space. This innovative serpentine element allows for flexible configurations to accommodate a variety of activities and to separate different program uses. Conceptually, and as a figural interior architectural element (or "direction"), this "livable bookworm" is a thick wall of books and bookshelves, incorporating small reading cubicles made of lapped plywood with bright colored surfaces. This living book-wall, with deep windows, provides a kind of "construction fence" that gives people a view into the library from other spaces within the building. There are inviting window seats that seem to say to those outside: "Come in to sit and read." The library space was designed for easy reconfiguration for various uses via hanging transparent theater screens that have been silkscreened with bold text and letters. The librarian and staff can configure these movable theater screens in different shapes to create spatial intimacy for small group activities while still maintaining visual supervision from outside the scrim space.

The creative quality of the transparent scrims is apparent in the way they can be successfully configured for both large and small group activities. Privacy is achieved by enclosing the space for small group storytelling, while expanding the scrims to a partial opening provides for staged activities for larger group assemblies. For large school events or community gatherings, the scrims are drawn all the way back and reconfigured to create one large communal space with movable bookshelves positioned in a tight, out-of-the-way cluster.

A number of custom-designed beanbag chairs provide flexible seating for students, adding to the fluidity of the space. Padded in bright colors, these chairs add a whimsical, animated quality to the space. The ease with which they can be moved allows them to be arranged to encourage community interaction.

The innovative renovation along with the relocation of the facility has brought new life to the school library. Openness, spatial freshness, and natural light combined with transparent materials and forms elevate the library's purpose and its place in the school community and neighborhood, bringing out the bookworm in all who enter.

1 Concept sketch
2 Inside the story telling area with the scrim curtains closed
3 Story telling area with scrim curtain

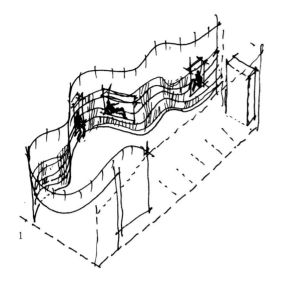

1

2

3

4 View of existing gymnasium before renovation
5 Concept sketch
6 General view of library from study area
7 Theater scrim curtain silk-screened with letters/words
  for the story telling area
8 Library floor plan, configured for individual study
9 Library floor plan, configured for large gatherings
10 View of library from entry

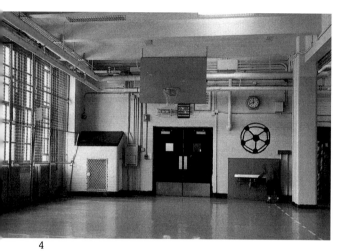

4

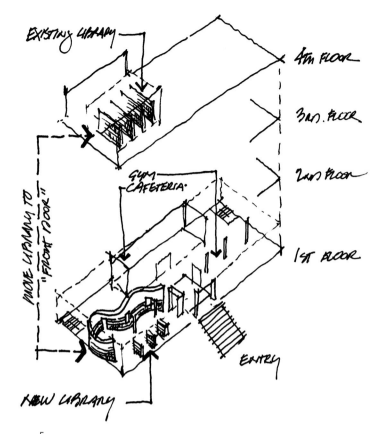

5

6

7

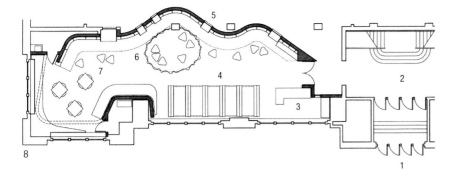

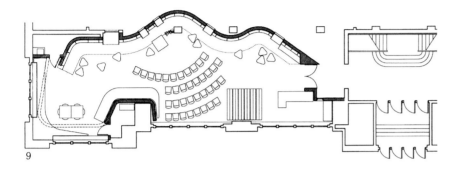

1	Building entry
2	Foyer
3	Librarians' work area
4	Deployable bookshelves
5	Corridor
6	Storytelling curtain
7	Rolling bean bag chairs

Urban Legend

Skidmore, Owings & Merrill, LLP

The Jin Mao Tower is China's tallest and one of the world's top-five tallest structures. Looking beyond its size to its details, however, shows a building that respects its surroundings and reflects its culture. Since its completion, Jin Mao has become a Shanghai landmark. Both socially and culturally, it represents the paradigm for synthesizing cultural identity with technology, both visually and systematically.

Jin Mao Tower is unique within its urban setting and makes a powerful statement; its exterior and interior reflect Chinese culture and its surroundings. The design incorporates the number eight, which the Chinese consider a lucky number, associated with prosperity, in its height and derivation of setbacks. The tower recalls historic Chinese pagoda forms, with setbacks that create a rhythmic pattern. Its metal and glass curtain wall reflects the constantly changing skies; at night its tower shaft and crown are illuminated. A successful design feature that brings the outside in by use of materials such as glass and steel, the network of horizontal bridges, and vertical circulation that eases movement through the vast open spaces in the building was designed to reflect the local setting. The zigzag bridge recollects the Nine-Turn Bridge, a regional landmark,

and the suspended curved bridges pay homage to a major suspension bridge over the Huang Pu River that flows through Shanghai. The colors yellow, blue, and red are used as accents for orientation and wayfinding throughout the vast space. A simple palette of warm, quiet hues is incorporated into the lobby's travertine flooring and walls to create a sense of serenity and balance. A major objective for the interior spaces in the tower was to establish a sense of harmony and unity as well as a sense of equilibrium in the complex and vast public spaces, which include retail spaces, the lobby, and an observatory.

China's population density and aspirations for a better living environment have, over the past several decades, driven local planners, engineers, and architects to devise ways to produce high-density urban forms that also exhibit high quality. The design of the Jin Mao Tower addresses the concern for a better environment and a high quality product within one structure.

The flow of symbolism and cultural expression throughout its highly technological design distinguishes the Jin Mao Tower. It is a building with a strong response to its surroundings and local culture that emits an inner beauty through its striking design.

Opposite:
   Upward-looking view from atrium

3

4

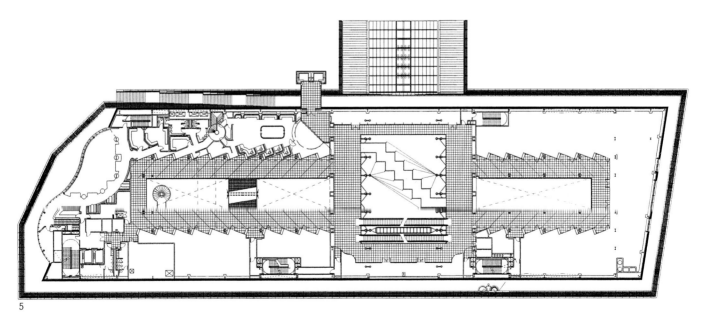

5

Opposite:
    Public circulation area
3   Podium interior
4   Public circulation area
5   Podium floor plan

6 Public circulation area
7 Elevator waiting area
8 Side view of atrium
9 Building exterior as seen through podium

6

7

8

9

10

10   Observation deck
11   Escalators

11

12

12   Public space in podium
Opposite:
    Building exterior

More and more, contemporary architects believe the effectiveness of a design solution is measured not only by its aesthetic outcome but also by client satisfaction and, more importantly, by the impact of the design on the client. Especially when it comes to interiors, the design solution is driven by client needs and is often measured by client satisfaction.

Although project outcome is not the only way to evaluate the success of a project, it is becoming more and more important as architects strive to explain the value of the design process to their clients. In-depth evaluations of completed projects often demonstrate that thoughtful design based on insight about the client's strategic goals does indeed lead to success on many levels. The four projects profiled in this chapter exemplify different metrics for success but for each the outcome is clearly measurable. Each project also demonstrates the significance of the design process in achieving the client's goals.

The effectiveness of a project can be measured in many ways. Understanding what must be measured and how to measure it should be determined at the beginning of a project. The key to success is to have a strong vision of what is most important to the client. Tying in strategic goals with financial goals is also key, but if the strategy is sound the financial goals usually follow. The architect's role is to understand the client's goals and to translate opportunities and constraints into a three-dimensional design solution.

In the case of Seiji Ozawa Hall, the Boston Symphony Orchestra wanted a community space to celebrate music. The client's measurable goals were to create a room that was acoustically significant and to accommodate a particular-sized audience in a unique venue. Throughout the process, the architect strove to understand just what vernacular cues and acoustical characteristics could be combined to create such a place. Performances by world-class music professionals in the hall's first 10 years have been evaluated by the musicians, arts critics, and audiences. What better way to measure the successful outcome of any endeavor?

Sometimes the vision for a project is strong, yet the outcome is unclear. In the case of the Chicago Tribune Pressroom, the client/architect team ventured into unexplored realms. The developing digital culture of the Tribune led to a marked change from how the newspaper staff had operated in the past. This called for new ways of defining space, creating layouts, and using technology and light. The project team explored possible solutions together, allowing the architect to lead the creative process and become a trusted business adviser to the organization. The design solution was successful in many measurable ways, but also in many immeasurable ones. The bottom-line savings to the owner created by reduced space needs was clearly the best evidence of financial gain. The fact that a project that set new standards for digital operations and infrastructure solutions also saved money was an added benefit.

Perhaps the greatest value of the project is that the design highlights the contrast and the connections between interactive media and publishing: the space represents the future of the organization.

What is it that makes a space successful? Sometimes it's giving people what they expect; sometimes it's exceeding their expectations. For the First Presbyterian Church of Encino, it was both. Understanding the nature of those who will use a building and the depths of their needs gives an architect special insight from which to propose design solutions. Beyond the basic constraints of schedule, budget, and cost, the dynamic power of architecture is its ability to invigorate and inspire clients. For the First Presbyterian of Encino, the architect took a simple concept and expanded it to encompass both physical and spiritual needs. By understanding the transformative power of light and its tie to religious and architectural spaces, the architect carefully molded a design solution that exceeded the expectations of the congregation. The success of this project was measured by the building committee and client testimonials and a noteworthy increase in membership.

"Image is everything." This statement reflects the visual standard set by advertising at the beginning of the 21st century. This standard has crossed into architectural interiors as clients become more and more engrossed with the trappings of image and its relationship to success. An organization's external image has become recognized as a way to strengthen and enhance the business mission. Look at the case of Group Goetz Architects (GGA) Design Studio. The firm's

increases in new client commissions, profitability, and staff recruitment can all be directly connected to the working environment in its new offices.

When an organization ties its goals, corporate culture, and marketing to a carefully conceptualized image, it bolsters its probability for success. Businesses are run by employees and their ability to sell their products and services. In architecture practice especially, the firm needs to represent what it sells: design based on function as well as aesthetics. In addition, to attract top talent, a business needs to build and maintain a pleasing and inspiring work environment. GGA did both of these things in parallel. Its success began as an aesthetic goal and became a financial boon.

Whether it's the impact on the bottom line of business, as in the GGA offices, or the "best of the best" ranking of a cultural arts facility such as the Seiji Ozawa Hall, it is the desire of both the owner and the architect to quantify the success of a project. Conclusions can be clearly drawn about the success of each of the projects featured in this chapter. Whether measured through client testimonials, employee satisfaction ratings, financial evaluations, or increases in use or attendance, each project surpassed the achievement of a pleasing aesthetic solution. It is the success of the designers in achieving a comprehensive solution that addresses the client's requirements in an aesthetically pleasing way that makes these projects stand out.

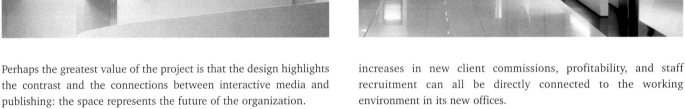

Client Satisfaction

A Room for Music

Seiji Ozawa Hall at Tanglewood, Lenox, Massachusetts

William Rawn Associates, Architects, Inc.
Kirkegaard Associates, Acousticians

Build a room for music—a simple request that had a simple solution but required a complicated journey to deliver. The outcome of this design project was a space created specifically for the enjoyment of music, but it evolved into much more. It became a room with a view, from inside to out, from outside to in; it became an experience of joy, a labor of love to complete, and a lasting legacy for the Boston Symphony Orchestra. The hall was named in honor of Seiji Ozawa, music director of the Boston Symphony Orchestra from 1973 to 2002. The postoccupancy evaluation of this project is a testimony to the success of team problem-solving. The measurable outcome is the facility's outstanding reputation and overall fame, which is evidenced, beyond its playbill of music greats, by its demonstrated value to patrons, students, and performers.

In 1989, when the Boston Symphony Orchestra Trustees Building Committee selected architect William Rawn to design their new summer concert hall at Tanglewood Music Center, they put a great deal of faith in a young architect who exhibited the sensitivity and resolve to work with the client in achieving a noble goal. The committee's dream was to create, in Rawn's words, "a room for music" in the tradition of other great performance spaces, with an acoustical excellence that would create a community of sound between the orchestra and an audience of 1,200.

The project was sited in the rolling hills of the former Highwood estate in Lenox, Massachusetts, site of the Tanglewood Music Center. Home to the Berkshire Symphonic Festival since the early 1930s, Tanglewood was a complex of studios, lecture halls, a library, and an amphitheater. The new concert hall would replace an old theater-concert hall completed in 1941, which had fallen into disrepair. The vision for the new facility entailed a sympathetic structure nestled into the hilly landscape that could accommodate a lawn audience and take advantage of the area's natural beauty.

Rawn spent most of the first five weeks of the project absorbing the character and ambience of Tanglewood and getting to know the students, orchestra, and management. His team talked with key figures from the BSO Board of Trustees, Tanglewood's administration, maestros, and musicians and sat in on rehearsals and concerts. Rawn found a "place of remarkable New England self-restraint" and was struck by the intensity of the students' musical experience. He also spent time researching more than ten of the most important performance halls from the 19th century, including Amsterdam's Concertgebouw and Vienna's Musikvereinssaal. Rawn toured, measured, and sketched these facilities with acoustician Lawrence Kirkegaard. Although the architect's primary interest lay in the spatial quality of the halls, he was observant of their acoustical solutions as well.

The solution Rawn proposed for Tanglewood was based on the concept of a New England meeting house: the hall would not be an auditorium, but more of a gathering space where the performers and audience could celebrate the community of live music. The audience would sit on three sides, with a big opening at the rear of the shoebox-shaped building. The lawn sloping away from this opening could accommodate hundreds more listeners.

The architecture of the building derives its form and materials not only from the local vernacular, but also from the acoustical requirements of such a space. The rectangular plan, the equivalent of a triple cube in volume, was a tried-and-true solution used in many of the successful concert halls Rawn had visited. The building is made up of an outer brick and block shell, which holds the sound and resonates to the low-frequency bass response, and an interior of timber and other wood elements; the platforms, balconies, and arcades are constructed of fir, cedar, teak, and reused heavy timbers. The arrangement of the arcades and the grid motif of the interior balcony railings and panels give the space a sense of human scale and create the reflection necessary for acoustical clarity. Depth and articulation were key factors in the design of the ceiling as well.

The collaboration of architect and acoustician has earned Ozawa Hall a rating as one of the top four concert halls in the United States and one of the top six halls built in the 20th century. It is ranked in the top 13 concert halls in the world. This ranking is based on interviews and questionnaires with conductors, music critics, and concert aficionados. Robert Campbell of the *Boston Globe* reported that Rawn and Kirkegaard developed a "give-and-take working

Opposite:
View of stage and north balconies

relationship in which each seemed to optimize the other's goals." The structure incorporates the massive walls required of a concert hall, yet suggests a remarkable lightness of structure. The wood grilles of the interior, necessary to blend and disperse sound, are designed as handsome architectural details such as coffers, bays, and crenellations.

According to Peter A. Brooks, chairman of the BSO Board of Trustees, Ozawa Hall is known as a "warm, inviting place that captures the democratic spirit of New England." The facility celebrated its 10th anniversary in 2004; over the first decade, its concerts became so popular that the concert hall enjoys an at- capacity audience for the entire season. The hall continues to accommodate the inventiveness of the Berkshire Music Festival and has housed dance performances as well. Patrons congregate in the arcades during intermission, taking advantage of the warm summer evenings and soft breezes. From almost any seat, inside or out, attendees can see sky, green trees, and lawn. The human qualities of intimacy and intensity in the "room" are part of the successful concert experience. Best of all, Ozawa Hall has been home to world-class musicians and performers and continues to inspire the Tanglewood Music Center students with the intensity and excellence of spirit and place that it provides.

2

2 Detail of west portal and exterior balcony looking into the hall
3 View of interior north side balcony through the portal at night

3

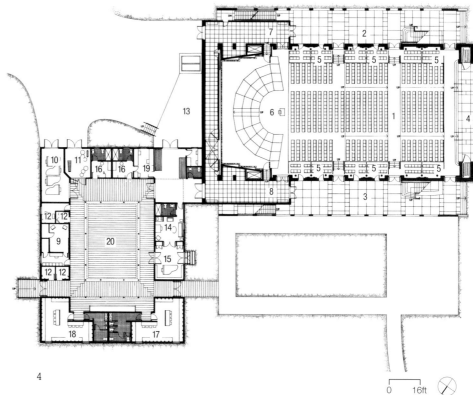

1   Auditorium main floor
2   Foyer, right
3   Foyer, left
4   Portal
5   Loge boxes
6   Concert platform
7   Platform wing, right
8   Platform wing, left
9   TMC sound booth and recording suite
10 Piano storage
11 Percussion storage
12 Practice room
13 Loading dock
14 Conductor's dressing room
15 Green room/recording booth
16 Guest soloists' dressing room
17 Musicians' changing room, female
18 Musicians' changing room, male
19 Music library and orchestra manager office
20 Open court/arcade/orchestra green room

4

0   16ft

4   Main level floor plan
5   The stage viewed from the portal at dusk
Opposite:
    View from the arcade into the hall

5

7 View of the stage with a chamber group
8 Detail toward the portal from the first floor balcony
9 Stage view from a loge box
10 Longitudinal section

7

8

9

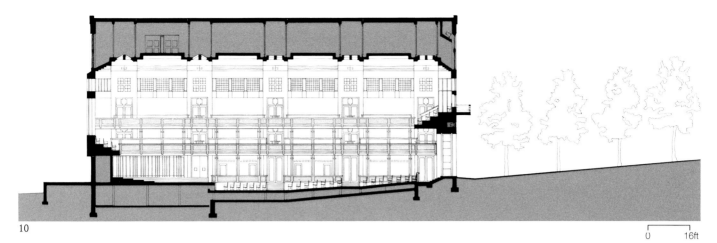

10

0   16ft

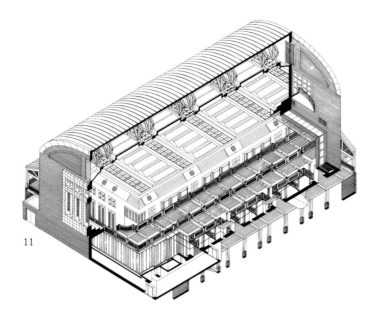

11

12

13

14

11 Dual axonometric of hall
12 Northwest elevation at dusk with a lawn audience
13 Detail of south wall, loges, and balconies
14 Stage detail toward southeast balconies
15 Structural concept—interpenetrating timber frame above
   acoustic shell/masonry box

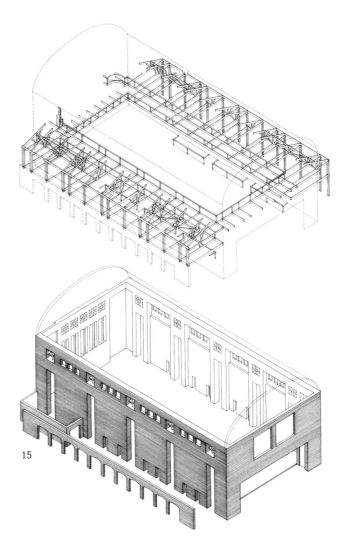

15

16

17

16 View from first floor balcony toward the south lawn
17 Detail of northwest stair opening and ceiling

Net Space

Perkins+Will

In 1999 the Tribune Company sought a dynamic space for Tribune Interactive, its new Internet division, after decades of providing successful media services in newspapers, radio, and television. As a natural next step, the company had chosen to add Internet services to the evolution of its communication group. Now, the Tribune wanted a space that would promote the youthful, tech-savvy side of the company while advancing the collaboration of the media group as a whole. After looking at numerous spaces in the city of Chicago, the company decided to transform the vacant pressroom located in the lower levels of Tribune Tower, and hired Perkins+Will as the architectural design consultant.

The client approached the project as the renovation of a windowless light industrial space into standard offices. Guided by Perkins+Will, however, a driving goal emerged to create a highly technical and modern environment while maintaining the historical context of the old pressroom. The rough-edged elements of the space, including structural concrete columns, were combined with sleek new features such as meeting rooms sheathed in Pilkington structural glass that stack like towers. The polished concrete floor of the entryway gives way to remnants of the old tracks used to move paper around the pressroom.

The abandoned pressroom, previously considered unusable, was essentially found space in the building. With no systems (elevators, sprinklers, or mechanical systems) up to code, the infrastructure needed to be overhauled. To accomplish this task, Perkins+Will chose to design a new "building within a building," making use of both its architectural and its interiors services.

A process of discovery continued throughout the renovation of the pressroom space; existing conditions quickly surfaced and drove some of the direction of the design. In the end, the architects came to an asymmetrically organized design—two floors on one side of the room and three floors on the other. The central space on the lower level was kept as an open zone, free of workstations, allowing it to serve as a "great room" for functions.

The lack of natural lighting available at the lower level presented a challenge. Lighting solutions were adapted for ceilings of various heights: 10 feet, 20 feet, and 32 feet. The lower ceilings are washed with light from custom-made indirect light fixtures. The middle level is lighted with high-bay pendant fixtures, some with fluorescent and some with halogen bulbs. The 32-foot ceilings in high-bay areas are dramatically illuminated with halogen theatrical fixtures. The glass towers of meeting rooms, lit from the inside, act as glowing light sources. Because of its reflective quality, glass was used extensively and strategically in the windowless spaces to magnify the perception of light. The transparent of the glass towers also serve as a metaphor for the Internet division's open, communicative work culture.

By leveraging the financial planning, business development, and design development goals for the project, the client/architect team created an environment that supports the Tribune's strategic goals of exploring the Internet medium to define the Tribune's online publishing opportunities and create a vibrant and profitable business. A number of measures reinforce the success of the project in achieving these goals.

The design of this facility allows for increased opportunities of cross-pollination by placing the editorial staff of four separate Web sites close together. Teams now have greater access to one another, encouraging them to share Web development experiences and suggestions; as a result, stronger content and design can be found on all the Web sites. Location of the Web staff and the newspaper's editorial staff in the same building also provides the Web teams with quick access to breaking news stories and knowledge of deadlines. This familiarity enables quick posting of stories online.

The new environment allows the Internet division to organically develop its professional, energetic, and open culture. The low-walled workstations encourage quick communication, and white boards provide an outlet for impromptu diagramming and posting of project timelines. Incorporation of both enclosed meeting spaces and open areas provide relaxed spaces for creative thinking and dialogue. The "great room" area at the center of the division's offices acts as a large meeting space for employees to gather and celebrate developments and successes.

Opposite:
West view of the typical three-level office tower within the structure

2

One project benefit is the elimination of lease costs. Assuming comparable rent at $25 per square foot and 94,000 square feet of space, lease costs would be approximately $2.35 million per year. In fewer than ten years, the Tribune will recoup its full investment cost.

The contrast between the new environment of Tribune Interactive and the old pressroom in which it stands highlights both the similarities and the differences between new media and traditional publishing. This contrast is communicated to recruits, who are often taken on a tour of the new space to demonstrate the continually evolving nature of media. The space also acts as a metaphor for the Tribune's commitment to embracing new media and a new approach to work. Users describe increased satisfaction with the space and spend more time in the environment. Nicknamed the "Digital Pressroom," the space acts as a magnet, pulling together employees from both within and outside the division.

Exposed ladder racks carrying cables allow easy access for maintenance and adaptation of wiring (for computer monitors and televisions) at much less cost than other wiring configurations. The client estimates this feature creates a cost savings of $40,000 per month. Voice over Internet Protocol (VoIP) presents a savings of $100,000 over traditional cable wiring costs and greatly reduces the cost of moving an employee within the office. These costs are approximately $125 per person with cable wiring, but with VoIP there is no cost to move, add, or change an employee's location within the space, again lending flexibility to the work environment. With uniform workstations and fully active network ports throughout the space, employees can easily relocate without IT assistance as project teams evolve.

This innovative project transformed a lower-level pressroom into 90,000 square feet of vibrant workspace for the Tribune Company's Internet division. The modern, open office environment contains 280 workstations, several open and enclosed team rooms, conference rooms, and a two-level fitness center. Breakout and pantry facilities are located throughout the new work environment. Space in the Tribune Interactive office is now highly sought after within the company and is used by the Tribune's entire media group.

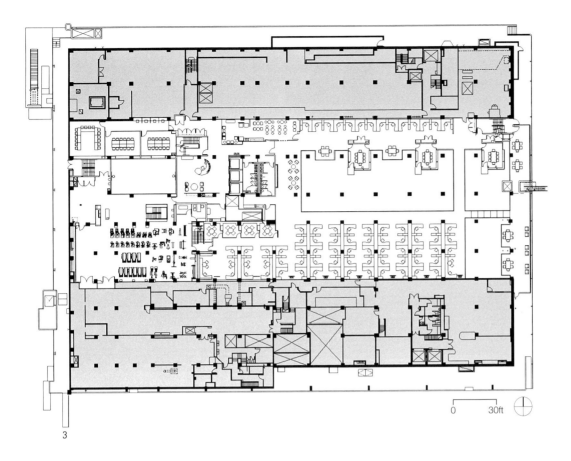

3

4

5

6

6 View through the office towers
7 The three-level structure viewed from the ground-level entry
8 Detail showing the integrated framework of the handrail/cabling distribution

8

7

Cupping Hands

First Presbyterian Church of Encino, California

Abramson Teiger Architects

The cupping of hands in prayer—a simple gesture, an expression of faith, and a metaphor of form—was the inspiration for the physical changes to the First Presbyterian Church of Encino. Pastor J. Malcolm Laing was looking to renovate a 1950s church building in decline as a means of invigorating his congregation. The architect was looking for an uplifting, enlightened concept to create a sacred place, one that "was small enough for intimacy to remain, yet large enough for silence to echo." What they produced together was indeed a miraculous transformation of spirit and place, one with positive, measurable outcomes for the congregation.

The goals for the renovation were to significantly improve the quality of illumination and to develop a form that would create a greater sense of closeness and reverie. The original church building, a typical 1954 A-frame structure, with a somber interior featuring tapered glulam columns of dark-stained wood.

Before the transformation, the nave was a traditionally axial and hierarchical form in which congregants gathered in a dark space apart from the pastor and choir. The new design brought forward and lowered the floor of the chancel and reorganized the pews in the round, creating a more embracing and participatory space. "Members and visitors alike have expressed the joy of the inclusive setting," according to Marilyn and Don Fetherolf, corporate secretary and finance officer of the church, respectively.

The entire ceiling was transformed into a sculptural volume, formed by offsetting two irregular, curved planes lit by a combination of natural and man-made light. The design team drew inspiration for these facing forms, which shelter the sanctuary, from early Christian depictions of the mother of Christ with her cupping hands. The two planes also hide the sources of light, which seem to pool in pockets, feathering out from the sides of the space. The coloration of the light is subtly different on each face, warmer on the south face than on the north. The effect of the natural light changes over time and is both fragile and powerful.

Light has long been used to shape religious spaces. Light filters through stained glass in medieval cathedrals and through controlled openings in small chapels such as Notre Dame du Haut in Ronchamps, France. According to Kenneth Chang, chair of the building committee, "the darkness [in the Encino church] was lifted with light from skylights filtering through canopies of cloud panels." The exceptional use of light, form, and symbol creates an architecture that inspires worshipers.

The architect of the First Presbyterian renovation considered the use of light a key design element. "The dynamic and transformative character of natural light heightens the sense of the ecstatic, of being brought into the revelation of divine grace and religious wisdom. Light is shaped in three movements that take the worshiper along a procession. The first movement is at the narthex, the entrance to the house of God, which filters in from above; its source is not evident. There is a suggestion of a space beyond, yet the main sanctuary is seen only through glimpses. The second movement corresponds to the main worship space. The congregation is illuminated by large openings to the north, which fill the sanctuary with tender light representative of God's love and charity. Sources from the south are low, creating a common horizon of more brilliant light illuminating the congregation, the community of man. The third movement is the most brilliant and the most varied. Only here does light flow directly down the curved surfaces that shape the sanctuary, finally illuminating the full form of the church."

Fourteen skylights, some hidden, along with incandescent theater fixtures in sheltered pockets and fluorescent cove lighting, strategically control the illumination. This configuration creates a symphony of light that is varied and continually changing. The effect leads the eye to the back of the chancel where an elongated cross rises above the altar.

The congregation hoped the renovation would help increase membership, particularly among young adults. This goal was accomplished in several ways. The design uses a white-on-white color palette that provides a contemporary backdrop for weddings. The church is open for weddings to both members of the congregation and to non-members. The latter group generated new members who returned for Sunday services because they liked the atmosphere of the church.

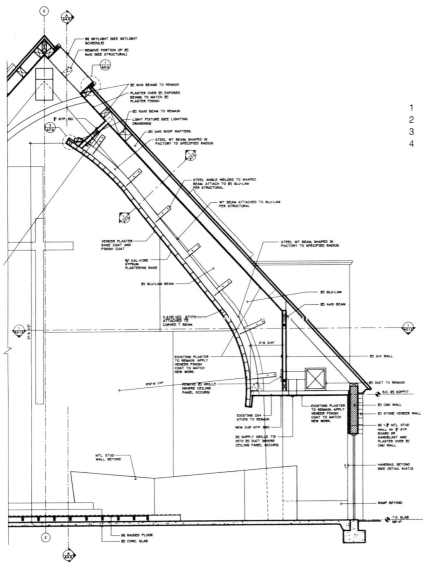

1 Roof section
2 View of choir seating, baptismal bowl, and communion table
3 Exterior view of church front façade at twilight
4 View from the community seating toward the chancel

1

2

3

4

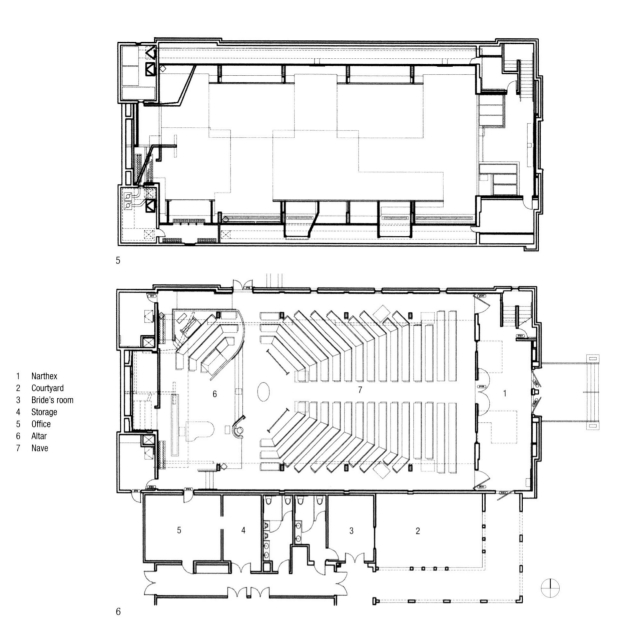

5

1 Narthex
2 Courtyard
3 Bride's room
4 Storage
5 Office
6 Altar
7 Nave

6

7

An increase in the attendance at weekly services is also the result of the intense spiritual nature of the space after the renovation. When people are in the sanctuary, their spirits are lifted; that alone keeps them coming back. Pastor Malcolm Laing states, "There has been a very noticeable return of visitors who are looking for a new congregation to join, resulting in a 20 percent increase in membership."

It is the religious experience that elevates the architecture of the renovated building and differentiates it from its previous form. According to Pastor Laing, "The remodeling of our sanctuary accomplished exactly what we had asked … a space that was light, uplifting, and welcoming … a space that physically manifested worship as a celebration in which all participate with the Eucharist, Baptism, and the Cross as the central focus … a space that felt holy. As people now enter our sanctuary for the very first time, their mouths fall open in awestruck appreciation. And, more importantly, they return again and again. The design, seating, acoustics, and multimedia capability have imbued our worship with renewed enthusiasm, greater energy, and stronger unity—pastors and people feel part of all that is taking place with all their senses engaged in creative ways … the sanctuary says, 'This is the community of new possibilities where awesome worship is an every-Sunday experience.' "

8

9

10

11

Sudden Impact

GGA Architects Design Studio, Washington, D.C.

Group Goetz Architects

Group Goetz Architects (formerly Greenwell Goetz Architects) acted as its own client in the design and build-out of its 25,500-square-foot studio in Washington, D.C. The firm's previous office was too small and its design too rigid. It lacked the space to accommodate how the architects worked best, and the space it did have neither expressed the firm's evolving culture nor represented its vision and values.

The design concept for the new offices was rooted in the firm's mission: to create workplace environments that support business goals, meet user needs, and enhance the overall quality of work life. In their work for leading corporations, the architects had noted a parallel between the evolution of new ways of working and the design of new types of workplaces.

For Group Goetz Architects (GGA), as well as its clients, the static format of the traditional office was giving way to alternative workplace settings tailored to accommodate evolving organizational models. As members of an entrepreneurial firm, the architects were rethinking how they provided services and sought for ways to enable office facilities to add profit and value. They were increasingly aware that the decisions they made about facilities and the design of the physical workspace would have many ramifications, particularly on the firm's abilities to stay competitive and to recruit and maintain top talent.

The architects wanted their environment to express what they believed in and what they extolled for their clients: design decisions based on functional aesthetics. This concept encompasses pragmatic considerations—flexibility, adaptability, ergonomics, appropriateness of materials, environmental comfort, and technology integration—as well as less tangible, though no less essential, concerns—image, pride in one's work, and a sense of community.

To support the work of the firm, the new space had to be flexible, allowing for frequent rearrangement of people as business objectives and projects dictated but avoiding a warehouse look or a sea of workstations. Choosing furniture and installing lighting with high ergonomic standards; delineating zones for clients, studios, and production efforts; and designing a space that is a creative and stimulating place to work were also project goals. The architects planned an interior with overlapping zones and few fixed walls to encourage a flow of energy. The zones are subtly identified by the placement of objects and lighting and the judicious use of curves.

The architects tackled issues of community and private space, along with connections to technology, information, clients, and colleagues. The systems furniture supports individual work areas that are arranged in quads to encourage a teamwork style. Movable partitions and workstations allow for mentoring, while living areas, a cappuccino bar, and a wine bar invite people to come together in a friendly way.

The architects employed large windows on the north, south, and west to capture available natural light. Despite the 41-foot bays in the original space, the architects were able to achieve huge columnless expanses. The center of the office space is densely populated with functional spaces, but the layout is more open toward the outside edges as the space expands into the city vistas.

For the most part, the lighting in the studio is indirect, using minimal task lighting. It is the lighting in the specialty spaces—the client-centered entry, reception, and living areas as well as the conference areas—that distinguishes these offices. Light is used as an architectural element: fluorescent tubing is inset as sculpture, while quad lamps with color gels create saturated, gradually shifting color rhythms that define and articulate planes.

With their expanded space, GGA increased staffing levels in an extremely tight and highly competitive labor market. Of the new employees hired, 80 percent said in post-hiring interviews that the new offices were the major factor in their choice of a place of employment. Ten percent reported the offices were the sole factor in their decision-making process.

In the first quarter of 2000, the firm earned its largest first-quarter revenue ever, a 56 percent increase over the previous year, with a profit margin increase of 400 percent. The win/loss ratio of projects won when potential clients had toured the space increased by 500 percent. On two occasions, a potential client hired the design firm before even leaving the reception area.

After the initial cost of moving into the space and of hiring and training a significant number of new staff members, GGA realized its most profitable year in the final quarter of 1999. The design for its new offices clearly met the firm's ambition of creating a workplace that supports business goals, meets user needs, and enhances the overall quality of work life.

1

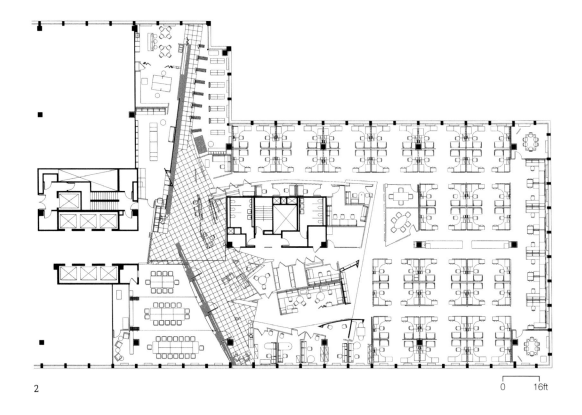

2

0   16ft

3

4

5

2 Floor plan
3 View of reception area from elevator lobby
4 Reception area viewed from an articulated opening
5 Building exterior
6 View of entrance to design studio from reception area

6

7

8

7　Conference room entrances and ante-area
　　viewed from the reception area
8　View of gallery and library
9&10　Cappuccino bar detail
11　View of the design studio and private offices
　　from the conference ante-area

9

10

11

AIA Honor Award for Interior
Architecture Recipients, 1994–2004

1994

A Connecticut Residence
(Single-family residence)
Greenwich, CT
Architect: Elliott + Associates Architects (interior) and
H.T. Graves & Associates (exterior)

Lawson/Westen House
(Single-family residence)
Los Angeles, CA
Architect: Eric Owen Moss Architects

Arrow International Inc.
(Office)
Reading, PA
Architect: Kallman McKinnell & Wood;
Stephanie Mallis, Interior Designer

Seafirst Gallery
(Cultural)
Seattle, WA
Architect: NBBJ

The John Tishman Auditorium
(Cultural)
New York, NY
Architect: Prentice & Chan, Ohlhausen

Adelbert Hall Administration Building
(Office)
Cleveland, OH
Architect: R.M.Kliment & Frances Halsband Architects

Knoll International Showroom
(Retail)
Frankfurt, Germany
Architect: Studios Architecture

The Icehouse
(Retail)
San Francisco, CA
Architect: Swatt Architects

1995

JPBT Headquarters
(Office)
Miami, FL
Architect: Carlos Zapata Design Studio
Associate Architect: Una Idea

Limelight Production
(Office)
Los Angeles, CA
Architect: Franklin D. Israel Design

Caroline's Comedy Night Club
(Recreational)
New York, NY
Architect: Haigh Architects

Graff Pay-Per-View
(Office)
New York, NY
Architect: Kathryn McGraw Berry

Public Bathrooms: Boston Center for the Arts
(Other)
Boston, MA
Architect: Kennedy & Violich Architects
Associate Architect: Arrowstreet, Inc.

Private Residence with Office/Gallery for the Lee Foundation
(Single-family residence)
St. Helena, CA
Architect: Kuth Ranieri; Jim Jennings Architecture

Center for the Arts Theater at Yerba Buena Gardens
(Cultural)
San Francisco, CA
Architect: Polshek & Partners Architects

Baruch College, Newman Library & Technology Center
(Library)
New York, NY
Architect: Davis, Brody & Associates, LLP

David Saul Smith Union at Bowdoin College
(College/university)
Brunswick, ME
Architect: Hardy Holzman Pfeiffer Associates
Associate Architect: Barba Architecture & Preservation

Christina Development Office
(Office)
Malibu, CA
Architect: Kanner Architects

The Lighthouse Headquarters
(Office)
New York, NY
Architect: Mitchell/Giurgola Architects

Guilford of Maine Design Studio & Showroom
(Cultural/retail)
Webster, MA
Architect: Robert Luchetti Associates

Gardner Residence
(Single-family residence)
Chicago, IL
Architect: Valerio Dewalt Train Associates

Bottega Venetta
(Retail)
Boston, MA
Architect: Francois deMenil Architects
Associate Architect: Bergmeyer Associates

Dillingham Hall
(Cultural)
Honolulu, HI
Architect: Hardy Holzman Pfeiffer Associates

New Victory Theater
(Cultural)
New York, NY
Architect: Hardy Holzman Pfeiffer Associates

Meyocks & Priebe Advertising
(Office)
West Des Moines, IA
Architect: Herbert Lewis Kruse Blunck Architecture

Praxair Distribution
(Office)
Ankeny, IA
Architect: Herbert Lewis Kruse Blunck Architecture

Root House
(Single-family residence)
Ormond Beach, FL
Architect: Pasanella + Klein Stolzman + Berg Architects, P.C.

Delano Hotel
(Hotel)
Miami Beach, FL
Architect: Phillippe Starck; PMG Architects

Tokyo International Forum
(Convention center)
Tokyo, Japan
Architect: Rafael Viñoly Architects

Bow Truss Studio/Game Show Network
(Other)
Culver City, CA
Architect: Steven Ehrlich Architects

Henri Beaufour Institute, USA
(Office)
Washington, D.C.
Architect: William & Dynerman Architects

The Salad Bowl
(Restaurant)
New York, NY
Architect: Boyd Associates

New Hearth Showroom
(Retail)
New York, NY
Architect: Centerbrook Architects, Mark Simon

Private Apartment
(Single-family residence)
New York, NY
Architect: Frank Lupo, Daniel Rowen, AIA

New Amsterdam Theatre
(Cultural)
New York, NY
Architect: Hardy Holzman Pfeiffer, Hugh Hardy

Massachusetts Institute of Technology School of Agriculture & Planning
(College/university)
Cambridge, MA
Architect: Leers Weinzapfel Associates, Jane Weinapfel

Manhattan Rooftop
(Single-family residence)
New York, NY
Architect: Shelton, Mindel & Associates, Lee F. Mindel, AIA
Associate Architect: Reed Morrison

Civic Opera House Renovation
(Cultural)
Chicago, IL
Architect: Skidmore, Owings & Merrill, LLP, Adrian D. Smith, FAIA

U.S. Court of Appeals
(Justice)
San Francisco, CA
Architect: Skidmore, Owings & Merrill, LLP, Craig Hartman

Wilkhahn North America Showroom
(Retail)
New York, NY
Architect: Skidmore, Owings & Merrill, LLP, Neil Fankel, AIA

The Helen & Harry Gray Court-Wadsworth Athenaeum
(Cultural)
Hartford, CT
Architect: Tai Soo Kim Partners

Judith Nessier Residence
(Single-family residence)
Chicago, IL
Architect: Tigerman McCurry, Stanley Tigerman, FAIA

101 CityFood Café
(Restaurant)
New York, NY
Architect: Westfourth Architects, Valdimir Arsene, AIA

1999

Urban Interface Loft
(Single-family residence)
New York, NY
Architect: Dean/Wolf Architects, Kathryn Dean

Jil Sander & Ultimo Boutique
(Retail)
San Francisco, CA
Architect: Gabellini Associates, Michael Gabellini, AIA,
c/o Fran Puglisi

Jil Sander Showroom
(Retail)
Hamburg, Germany
Architect: Gabellini Associates, Michael Gabellini, AIA,
c/o Fran Puglisi

M.C. Ginsberg Objects of Art
(Retail)
West Des Moines, IA
Architect: Herbert Lewis Kruse Blunck Architecture

National Postal Museum
(Cultural)
Washington, D.C.
Architect: KCF/SHG, Inc., David R. H. King, FAIA

The Denver Central Library
(Library)
Denver, CO
Architect: Klipp Colussy Jenks DuBois Architects, Allison Cooper

Studio Residence
(Single-family residence)
Omaha, NE
Architect: Randy Brown Architects, Randy Brown, AIA

The Gagosian Gallery
(Cultural)
Beverly Hills, CA
Architect: Richard Meier & Partners, Richard Meier, FAIA

Little Village Academy
(School K-12)
Chicago, IL
Architect: Ross Barney Architects, Carol Ross Barney, FAIA

FILA Corporate Headquarters
(Office)
Sparks, MD
Architect: Shelton, Mindel & Associates, Lee Mindel, AIA

Central Park Residence
(Single-family residence)
New York, NY
Architect: Shelton, Mindel & Associates, Lee Mindel, AIA

2000

Ackerman McQueen Advertising Executive Office and Video Conferencing
(Office)
Tulsa, OK
Architect: Elliott + Associates Architects

Colleen B. Rosenblat Jewelry Showroom and Office
(Retail)
Hamburg, Germany
Architect: Gabellini Associates

Helmut Lange Boutique
(Retail)
New York, NY
Architect: Gluckman Mayner Architects

GGA Design Studio
(Office)
Washington, D.C.
Architect: Group Goetz Architects

San Francisco City Hall Improvement Project
(Civic)
San Francisco, CA
Architect: Heller Manus Architects
Associate Architect: Komorous Towy Architects and
Finger and Moy Architects

Farnsworth House Restoration
(Single-family residence)
Plano, IL
Architect: Lohan Associates (now Goettsch Partners)

SHR Perceptual Management Workspace
(Office)
Scottsdale, AZ
Architect: Morphosis

Oceanliner Dining Room and Lounge
(Restaurant)
Miami, FL
Architect: Shelton, Mindel and Associates

Fifth Avenue Duplex
(Single-family residence)
New York, NY
Architect: Shelton, Mindel and Associates

St. Jean Vianney Catholic Church Sanctuary
(Religious)
Baton Rouge, LA
Architect: Trahan Architects

Long Meadow Ranch Winery
(Single-family residence)
St. Helen's, CA
Architect: Turnbull Griffin Haesloop

Iwataya Passage
(Transportation)
Fukokashi, Japan
Architect: Walker Group/CNI

Seiji Ozawa Hall at Tanglewood
(Cultural)
Lenox, MA
Architect: William Rawn Associates

Petronas Twin Towers
(Mixed-use)
Kuala Lumpur, Malaysia
Architect: Cesar Pelli & Associates (now Pelli Clark Pelli Architects)

2001

Detroit Opera House
(Cultural)
Detroit, MI
Architect: Albert Kahn Collaborative
Associate Architect: JPRA Architects

SoHo Loft
(Single-family residence)
New York, NY
Architect: Architecture Research Office

Alliance Français de Chicago
(Institution)
Chicago, IL
Architect: DeStefano and Partners

Lucent Technologies
(Office)
Washington, D.C.
Architect: Group Goetz Architects

Radio City Music Hall
(Cultural)
New York, NY
Architect: Hardy Holzman Pfeiffer Associates

Herman Miller National Showroom
(Retail)
Chicago, IL
Architect: Krueck and Sexton

Jacobs Residence Subterranean
(Single-family residence)
Sherman Oaks, CA
Architect: Tighe Architecture

Reactor Films
(Office)
Santa Monica, CA
Architect: Pugh + Scarpa Architecture

Fitch O'Rourke Residence
(Single-family residence)
Washington, D.C.
Architect: Robert M. Gurney, FAIA

Higgins Hall Pratt Institute of Architecture
(College/university)
Brooklyn, NY
Architect: Rogers Marvel Architects, PLLC
Associate Architect: Ehrenkrantz and Eckstut Associates

New York Stock Exchange Trading Floor Expansion
(Institution)
New York, NY
Architect: Skidmore, Owings & Merrill, LLP
Associate Architect: Parson Main

Jin Mao Tower
(Office)
Shanghai, China
Architect: Skidmore, Owings & Merrill, LLP
Associate Architect: Shanghai Institute of Architectural Design and Research

2002

Qiora Store and Spa
(Retail)
New York, NY
Architect: Architecture Research Office

Old St. Patrick's Church
(Religious)
Chicago, IL
Architect: Booth Hansen Associates

TWBA/Chiat/Day Advertising
(Office)
Los Angeles, CA
Architect: Clive Wilkinson Architects

Rose Main Reading Room, New York Public Library
(Library)
New York City, NY
Architect: Davis Brody Bond, LLP

North House
(Single-family residence)
Oklahoma City, OK
Architect: Elliott + Associates Architects

Sticks, Inc.
(Office)
Des Moines, IA
Architect: Herbert Lewis Kruse Blunck Architecture

Chicago Tribune Pressroom
(Industrial)
Chicago, IL
Architect: Perkins+Will
Associate Architect: McClier Corporation

XAP Corporation
(Office)
Culver City, CA
Architect: Pugh + Scarpa Architecture

New International Terminal, San Francisco International Airport
(Transportation)
San Francisco, CA
Architect: Skidmore, Owings & Merrill, LLP; Del Campo & Maru;
Michael Willis Architects

Tsunami
(Restaurant)
Las Vegas, NV
Architect: Morphosis, Thom Mayne, AIA,

Smith-Buonanno Hall
(Cultural)
Providence, RI
Architect: William Kite Architects, Inc.

2003

Craft
(Restaurant)
New York, NY
Architect: Bentel & Bentel Architects/Planners

Architecture of R.M. Schindler Exhibit at MOCA
(Other)
Los Angeles, CA
Architect: Chu + Gooding Architects

South Court, New York Public Library
(Library)
New York, NY
Architect: Davis Brody Bond, LLP

ImageNet
(Office)
Oklahoma City, OK
Architect: Elliott + Associates Architects

Kate and Laurence Eustis Chapel
(Religious)
New Orleans, LA
Architect: Eskew+Dumez+Ripple

Central Synagogue
(Religious)
New York, NY
Architect: H³ Hardy Collaboration Architecture, LLC

Global Crossing Corporate Headquarters
(Office)
New York, NY
Architect: Lee H. Skolnick Architecture

Martin Shocket Residence
(Single-family residence)
Chevy Chase, MD
Architect: McInturff Architects

Lutèce
(Restaurant)
Las Vegas, NV
Architect: Morphosis

Collins Gallery
(Cultural/single-family residence)
West Hollywood, CA
Architect: Tighe Architecture

Gardner-James Residence
(Single-family residence)
New York, NY
Architect: Valerio Dewalt Train Associates

First Presbyterian Church of Encino
(Religious)
Encino, CA
Architect: Abramson Teiger Architects

American Meteorological Society Editorial Offices
(Office)
Boston, MA
Architect: Anmahian Winton Architects

Carol & Carl Montante Cultural Center
(Cultural center)
Buffalo, NY
Architect: Cannon Design

Pallota TeamWorks New Headquarters
(Industrial)
Los Angeles, CA
Architect: Clive Wilkinson Architects

NAI Exhibit-Silent Collisions: Morphosis Retrospective
(Other)
Rotterdam, The Netherlands
Architect: Morphosis

Co-Op Editorial
(Office)
Santa Monica, CA
Architect: Pugh + Scarpa Architecture

Academic Center for Student Athletes at Louisiana State University
(College/university)
Baton Rouge, LA
Architect: Trahan Architects

The Robinhood Foundation/NYC Public School 42, Queens Library
(Library)
Arverne, NY
Architect: Weiss/Manfredi

Winning Projects, 2000–04

2000

Colleen B. Rosenblat Jewelry Showroom and Office
Hamburg, Germany
Architect: Gabellini Associates

The setting for this renowned jewelry designer's showroom, accompanied by a studio, office, and small apartment, is a former carriage house in a historic section of Hamburg, Germany. The restored 4,500-square-foot interior of the shop parallels many of the client's designs: rough-cut stones in crisply crafted settings. Lit from within, the display cases present miniature *mise-en-scenès*, with a mixture of lighting methods that complement the white and yellow gold and intensely colored stones. For security, a sheet of laminated white glass over each display case conceals a locking mechanism; these sheets appear fluid, giving a levitating sensation of floating glass.

Helmut Lange Boutique
New York, New York
Architect: Gluckman Mayner Architects

This renovation of a 3,500-square-foot loft into a flagship boutique for Helmut Lang challenges both traditional retail planning and consumer experience. Launching a new image in New York, clothing designer, architect, and two well-known artists joined forces to create a unique retail space. The merchandising area sits at the rear of the store, separating it from the street, while the front space is a reception area. A full-height translucent glass wall draws the customer past an artist's installation into the main retail area. The perimeter walls are free of displays; they act as a simple blank backdrop, and a continuous skylight emphasizes the verticality of the space.

San Francisco City Hall Improvement Project
San Francisco, California
Architect: Heller Manus Architects
Associate Architects: Komorous Towy Architects and Finger and Moy Architects

The city of San Francisco funded improvements to transform its city hall into a modern, functioning office building. Included in the renovations were courtroom conversions, increased disability access, and installation of new HVAC systems. An interior feature that sparked wide attention was the reopening of the glass-and-steel light courts to the north and south of the rotunda, which had been removed in 1977. The light courts have been restored to their original beauty, once again admitting daylight into the 7,000-square-foot spaces on the main floor below. These areas have been returned to public use for staging events and exhibits.

SHR Perceptual Management Workspace
Scottsdale, Arizona
Architect: Morphosis

This 15,000-square-foot advertising agency was designed to reflect its mission: to redefine a client's identity by translating verbal information into physical form. The project reflects the contemporary workplace, where teamwork replaces traditional hierarchy in pursuit of greater innovation. The office is entered via a suspended steel bridge. A serpent-like structure—essentially an inhabited wall that sweeps and dips—begins at the reception area. The need for open and closed workplaces makes for a hybrid office. Each team maintains optimum connection without a loss of privacy. The creative teams occupy workspaces along the serpentine wall that open to the shared central design studio. Management and support staff occupy the perimeter of the space, where planes of glass replace the wall and doors are nonexistent.

Oceanliner Dining Room and Lounge
Miami, Florida
Architect: Shelton, Mindel and Associates

This project comprised designs for the dining room, atrium, and lounge aboard a major ocean liner, for which the architects drew on the art of shipbuilding. The dining room, a grand open-air salon, has a wood domed ceiling, a stainless steel-and-glass bridge, and a grand stainless steel-and-wood stair. Marine-blue, red, and gray cubist rugs differentiate the canal-like space. Materials in the atrium—a three-story bar—include stainless steel, structural glass, leather, perforated metal, and white glass. The lounge features undulating banquette seating; a bar of leather, steel, and glass; and a perforated metal-and-wood ceiling. Although they are separate, the three spaces present a conscious processional relationship.

Long Meadow Ranch Winery
St. Helen's, California
Architect: Turnbull Griffin Haesloop

The interior spaces of this small family winery and olive-pressing operation range from the production-oriented ground floor rooms and cave cellar to a workroom, conference room, and private office upstairs. The design embodies the spirit of wine and olive oil making, and the structure, including the earth walls and wood framing, is exposed throughout. The hose stations, power outlets, and plumbing fittings are detailed to bolt onto the earth walls, exposing the building systems. The plywood roof decking is stained the color of red wine, and the metal screens of the computer workstations echo the protective screen on the wine press.

Iwataya Passage
Fukokashi, Japan
Architect: Walker/Group CNI

This underground train station department store passageway is a public–private collaboration. The city of Fukuoka paid for the tunnel construction; the department store covered the cost of the passageway construction and interior finishes. The passageway features a water theme and a series of three pedestrian "bridges"— structures of steel, cable, and suspended glass. Several methods of indirect lighting achieve a softly luminous interior. Lumacite (translucent acrylic) creates light-reflective, shimmering effects, and the path has cable-suspended edge-lit glass at both ends. An interactive sound program mixes water sounds with recorded human voices reciting haiku. This passageway provides a needed modern service, but also suggests a contemporary version of the ancient city and evokes the lyrical character of water.

Petronas Twin Towers
Kuala Lumpur, Malaysia
Architect: Cesar Pelli & Associates (now Pelli Clark Pelli Architects)

These two 88-story office towers house an 863-seat concert hall, a science museum, an art gallery, and multi-story shopping; midway to the top, a sky bridge connects the towers. Each tower is set back six times as it ascends, and in the upper setbacks, the walls tilt toward the center, forming a geometric pattern based on Islamic traditions. The buildings' interiors feature local colors and traditional patterns and crafts that reflect the diverse culture of Malaysia. The concert hall incorporates a unique acoustic design in its perforated metal ceiling, which appears solid but is in fact acoustically transparent, allowing sound to travel to an upper ceiling, where seven movable panels adjust to create a range of acoustic environments.

2001

Alliance Française de Chicago
Chicago, Illinois
Architect: DeStefano and Partners

The Alliance Française de Chicago, housed in a Victorian townhouse, expanded its space by purchasing a former bank abutting the existing property at the rear garden and alley. The design plan fuses the two buildings into a campus of approximately 17,000 square feet that features a 150-person theater and a kitchen classroom for culinary instruction. The project reflects the French cultural value of preserving the best of the past while inserting dramatic contemporary work into the urban fabric, and the clearly contemporary, minimalist architecture of this project creates an almost museum-like environment. The architect sought to make clear distinctions between the contemporary and vintage structures so that visitors understand the layers of history that make up the facility.

Lucent Technologies
Washington, D.C.
Architect: Group Goetz Architects

Lucent Technologies wanted a high-profile presence in Washington, D.C. The design goals of the project included creating flexible, ergonomic workspaces; amenities such as a cafe and team rooms; and transient workstations for occasional use by staff members who spend most of their time out of the office. The company also wanted its offices to showcase the company's latest technology. The starkly glowing lobby epitomizes the sculptural nature of the interiors and demonstrates that light is essential to the appreciation of sculpture. The office design features aluminum—rigid, curving, or woven as a textile—as well as steel, glass, wood, and terrazzo. These materials have been pulled together into an inventive sculptural whole.

Radio City Music Hall
New York, New York
Architect: Hardy Holzman Pfeiffer Associates

When it opened in 1932, Radio City Music Hall was one of the most modern and beautiful theaters in the world; a celebration of American Modernism. By 1999, however, the theater had become a pale copy of its original splendor. A major restoration and renewal of the 500,000-square-foot complex was undertaken, including the grand foyer, the auditorium and its mezzanines, and the grand lounge. The architects recaptured the building's glamour using the bold patterns and finishes of the original carpeting, wall coverings, and upholstery fabrics. The murals were restored to their full brilliance and the original Deskey furniture and light fixtures were refurbished. The restoration also improved back-of-house areas, lighting systems, and theater technologies and adapted the building for television broadcasts.

Herman Miller National Showroom
Chicago, Illinois
Architect: Krueck and Sexton

Herman Miller sought to redesign and expand its 25,000-square-foot flagship furniture showroom in the Chicago Merchandise Mart. The architects drew on the technical, spatial, and aesthetic possibilities of glass and its translucency. The effect is a subtle flow of space, color, and light that dematerializes the ceiling into a series of luminous waves. This open approach to the design of the space provides flexibility for easy reconfiguration of the furniture. The ceiling system also offers an innovative way to resolve the design challenge of the typical open office; the result is a showroom elevated to the status of an exhibit gallery.

Jacobs Residence
Sherman Oaks, California
Architect: Tighe Architecture

This project required a 1,200-square-foot excavation on a steep hillside site. Working within regulations that prohibit alterations to the existing structure, the architect devised a terraced solution that satisfies the strict hillside code requirements. In this alternative to the traditional basement, multiple floor planes and angled white walls serve as a backdrop for the client's art collection and for the enjoyment of music. The large, cascading grand stair connects all the floors of the multi-tiered space, creating a unifying whole. A kitchenette is tucked below the shower. The entertainment room overlooks all levels to the landscape beyond.

Higgins Hall, Pratt Institute of Architecture
Brooklyn, New York
Architect: Rogers Marvel Architects PLLC
Associate Architect: Ehrenkrantz and Eckstut Associates

Higgins Hall at the Pratt Institute of Architecture has weathered four additions and two major fires. The most recent fire, in 1996, left a roofless brick masonry shell with many scarred windows. The wooden floors, timber lintels, two stairs, arched openings, and curved masonry walls all survived the fire, preserving a connection to the building's rich history. Major design goals were to reveal the poetry within the ruin and create an exciting workplace for architecture. Simple surfaces were applied to existing walls and strategically pulled away to reveal the building's past. New construction methods were developed that allowed eccentricities to stand out and be celebrated.

2002

Old St. Patrick's Church
Chicago, Illinois
Architect: Booth Hansen Associates

Irish immigrants built Old St. Patrick's Church in 1854. In this renovation, the architects incorporated technology to recreate and expand the building's historic artistry and Celtic heritage, employing the process of casting and the use of computerized craftsmanship. Complex architectural details and ornaments were fabricated by making multiple casts of either concrete or plaster from one mold. For such items as the baptismal font, chandeliers, and curved wood pews, computerized craftsmanship achieved intricate Celtic Renaissance details affordably with laser-cutting machines that use high-pressure water to fabricate details and ornaments from wood, stone, metal, and glass. This project marries modern technology and ancient craftsmanship.

TWBA/Chiat/Day Advertising
Los Angeles, California
Architect: Clive Wilkinson Architects

TWBA/Chiat/Day Advertising planned to relocate its offices to a space it envisioned as an "advertising city" constructed inside a large warehouse, where its 500 employees could be in one space. The project offered the architects the chance to develop a small city environment with multiple levels, green park space, landmark structures, an irregular "skyline," and distinct neighborhoods. To humanize the raw industrial space, traditional urban planning concepts of a city center, Main Street, neighborhoods, parks, alleys, civic functions, and building façades became design elements. After detailed research, a program was produced for an adaptable workstation solution. In June 1999, the patented workstation product became available from furniture dealerships.

North House
Oklahoma City, Oklahoma
Architect: Elliott + Associates Architects

This restored and renovated 1920's Italianate-style garage and servant quarters, in a neighborhood listed on the National Register of Historic Places, is located 50 feet north of the existing main house. The design concept grew from an understanding of the origins of Oklahoma as Indian territory and of the unique light of the place, as well as the work of North Losey, a well-known Oklahoma documentary photographer at the beginning of the 20th century, who caught both on film. The design for the interior of this structure honors the four sacred directions and the four lights, and this "light box" pays homage to Losey's work.

Sticks, Inc.
Des Moines, Iowa
Architect: Herbert Lewis Kruse Blunck Architecture

Sticks, Inc. is a rapidly growing artists' studio that specializes in contemporary art objects made from fallen timber and milled wood. The building, an assemblage of programmatic elements and building systems, is meant to stimulate production efficiency, growth, and operational flexibility. Its basic structural system is a pre-engineered steel frame and roof. The building envelope, of metal panels and tilt-up precast concrete, has been shifted off the steel frame, creating a display space along the east edge of the interior and a loggia along the west façade. Varying fenestration systems provide natural light essential to the artists. A collaborative effort between artists and architects, this project promotes a communal work environment.

Tsunami
Las Vegas, Nevada
Architect: Morphosis, Thom Mayne, AIA

When the architects conceived the design for the restaurant Tsunami, they began by having the existing restaurant space painted black to return the site to a generic box condition. They then used this "black box" as a backdrop for a two-dimensional, 100- by 100-foot printed surface, which they manipulated to define the restaurant's spaces. In a nod to simulated cultural identity and experience, the images on this design element form a dense collage representative of Asian culture. The design concept marries the figurative logic of drawing and the spatial logic of architecture.

2003

Architecture of R.M. Schindler Exhibit at MOCA

Los Angeles, California
Architect: Chu+Gooding Architects

In designing the R.M. Schindler exhibit at the Museum of Contemporary Art in Los Angeles, the architects sought to create a tactile, spatial backdrop for viewing the artist's work and to evoke his spirit of experimentalism without overt references or mimicry, all within a modest budget. The distance from the museum entry to the first gallery of the exhibition space is 20 feet. This first space prepares the viewer to focus on the small-scale, subtle drawings. The design resolves the conflict between the overwhelming size of the galleries and the small scale of the artwork and creates a display system that brings coherence to the variety of formats in the displayed artwork.

South Court, New York Public Library

New York, New York
Architect: Davis Brody Bond, LLP

This three-story infill structure is located in the south courtyard of the New York Public Library. Once an entrance for horse carriages, the $29-million addition reflects a major design goal of the project: it respects the historic 1911 Beaux Arts building yet achieves a sense of modernity. The entire structure is illuminated with skylights, and the floor is set back from the existing stone walls of the courtyard. The original foundation walls are exposed at the bottom of a glass staircase, which descends from the first floor to the auditorium. The upper floors are cantilevered and held back from the original walls by glass partitions, adding to the feeling of transparency.

ImageNet

Oklahoma City, Oklahoma
Architect: Elliott + Associates Architects

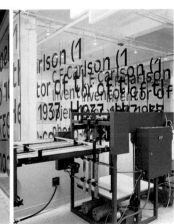

In redesigning its Oklahoma City copy center, the office systems and document-support company ImageNet wanted to share its company history and use the interior as both a sales and employee-recruitment tool. The interior of the resulting facility features vintage and rare typewriters as art objects and presents historical advancements in the business from typewriters to digital scanning. The space is organized so customers can tour and view the production and assembly process. When the project was completed, ImageNet secured a large scanning/imaging job from a major law firm—the single largest job in the company's history. When asked why they chose ImageNet, the law firm responded that they had appreciated knowing the company's history and had found the work space inventive, efficient, and organized.

Central Synagogue
New York, New York
Architect: H³ Hardy Collaboration Architecture, LLC

Constructed in 1872, this synagogue weathered a fire in 1998 that consumed the roof and most of its wooden truss supports. Although the resulting collapse and thousands of gallons of water used to put out the fire caused severe damage, the congregation chose to rebuild within the synagogue's historic walls. In addition to updating the building systems, nearly every surface in the synagogue was re-created to integrate old and new, including ornate plasterwork, woodwork, stencil painting, and encaustic tile flooring. Many hours of historical research were required to re-create this sacred space, as well as the services of more than 70 specialty firms and nearly 700 workers.

Global Crossing Corporate Headquarters
New York, New York
Architect: Lee H. Skolnick Architecture

For its new headquarters, this extranet communications firm chose several floors of an award-winning I.M. Pei-designed 1970's office building. The CEO-envisioned design focused on connectivity, speed, security, and cutting-edge technology. The design stripped all extraneous elements—partitions, hung ceilings, standard lighting, floor coverings, and added back only what was needed. The result is a 21st-century space in a classic 20th-century corporate envelope. Sculptures, lit internally by fiber-optic filaments, seem to float above work spaces and communal areas, providing continuity, fluidity, and a soft ambient glow. This representational concept of the neuron became so prominent a company symbol that it appears as an annual report cover design.

Kate and Laurence Eustis Chapel
New Orleans, Louisiana
Architect: Eskew+Dumez+Ripple

As part of Ochsner's "community of care" philosophy, this small interdenominational chapel serves the contemplative and spiritual needs of patients, families, and staff. Working collaboratively with a focus group of Ochsner staff and local artisans, the design team created a space to allow for flexible, non-permanent placement of specific religious iconography by introducing more universal themes of healing and reconciliation to engage visitors with the spiritual. Water is introduced in a manner that alludes to its healing, life-giving properties. Light, scale, proportion, and material treatments also serve to engage visitors with memories of the sacred. Three distinct spaces serve the programmatic needs of the project: the chapel, enveloped by a woven wood ceiling, provides seating for small groups, while two adjacent rooms are available for more intimate or private meditation.

Martin Shocket Residence
Chevy Chase, Maryland
Architect: McInturff Architects

The backyard of this 1920's foursquare catalog house in the
Washington, D.C. area housed a separate one-story building of
equal footprint, which had been built as a photographer's studio.
The architects integrated this room into the client's family life by
opening up the connection between the two buildings and giving
the resulting family room a strong orientation to the garden in the
side yard. A spare, modern aesthetic contrasts with and
complements the existing house. Steel windows, glass block for
privacy, and a column-free porch orient the room to the exterior.
The generous dimensions of the room allowed the architects to
articulate walls and ceiling by projecting surface planes into the
space without sacrificing function.

Collins Gallery
West Hollywood, California
Architect: Tighe Architecture

This project combines a public art gallery and a private home in
one space. The design challenge was to create a spacious gallery
within a relatively small building envelope. A new load-bearing
wall bisects the building on the diagonal. Two distinct zones were
created that differentiate the gallery from the residence and
separate the public from the private areas. The gallery's roof plane
was lifted to allow light in, and the resulting clerestory serves as
the main light source, eliminating the need for windows and
maximizing the wall surface available to display art. Sliding glass
partitions close the domestic rooms off from the gallery.

American Meteorological Society Editorial Offices
Boston, Massachusetts
Architect: Anmahian Winton Architects

The American Meteorological Society, headquartered in a historic mansion, expanded its operations into an attached carriage barn, which is now office space for 13 editors. The interior design of the new space was influenced by three primary elements and their relationship to each other: the carriage barn shell, new steel beams and perimeter plates, and an object-like mezzanine. Asymmetrically placed along the central axis of the barn, the mezzanine is a container for the workstations above and provides lighting and a sense of enclosure for the workstations below. In keeping with its original character, the barn features a simple, direct palette of materials: plywood, structural lumber, fiberglass panels, and raw, unpainted steel.

Carol & Carl Montante Cultural Center, Canisius College
Buffalo, New York
Architect: Cannon Design

This decommissioned 1926 church is a rare U.S. example of Byzantine-Lombardic architecture. The renovation transformed the building into a cultural center on a 2,500-student liberal arts college campus. The project called for a 600-seat, multipurpose space suitable for lectures, plays, and concerts. Infrastructure systems needed contemporary upgrades; most importantly, the acoustics needed to meet superior performance criteria. Because the volume of space under the dome was the source of historic acoustical problems, the design challenge was to introduce sound-reflecting surfaces within the domed volume while preserving the view of the striking mosaics. To solve this problem, the architects designed new constructed pieces to be inserted into the existing, undisturbed fabric of the building.

NAI Exhibit—Silent Collisions: Morphosis Retrospective
Rotterdam, The Netherlands
Architect: Morphosis

For the California architecture firm Morphosis, this exhibit at the Netherlands Architecture Institute was inspired in part by the firm's move from traditional drawing techniques to digital technologies, a transition that blurs the line between built form and process. The architects reconfigured the large open exhibition space, creating a central platform that transforms from views of the surrounding city to projection screens showing the work of Morphosis; the structural support for this space serves as the backdrop for further more traditional forms of the firm's work—models, drawings, and photographs. The horizontal layers in the design of the exhibit space reflected the surrounding cityscape, and the movement patterns created within the gallery were intended to pique the visitor's interest in the modern city as a site constantly in flux.

Academic Center for Student Athletes, Louisiana State University
Baton Rouge, Louisiana
Architect: Trahan Architects

Two objectives guided the architects of this renovation/adaptive reuse of a high school gym built in 1930: to retain its historical significance and to create an optimal learning environment. To meet these design goals, the design preserves the original appearance of the building's exterior and establishes a simple interior color and materials palette to encourage learning for today's students, whose fast-paced lives are full of distractions. The ceiling was raised and coffered in a consistent pattern, creating a unique experience from multiple viewpoints. The interior of the center emits a sense of discovery as students and other users move throughout the space.

Firm Profiles

This section presents brief biographies of the firms that received AIA Honor Awards for Interior Architecture from 2000 to 2004.

Abramson Teiger Architects
Culver City, California

Abramson Teiger Architects is led by Trevor Abramson, AIA, and Douglas Teiger, AIA, who strive for a constant balance of practical needs and dramatic artistic expression. The principals treat every project as an exercise in collaboration, with the client's design, scheduling, and financial goals at the center of consideration. The touchstone of the firm's design philosophy lies within the exploration of modernism and how it can inspire the people who dwell and work in architectural homes. The firm's architecture does not simply rest on its clean lines, but integrates light and air within structured spaces of material and form.

Albert Kahn Associates, Inc.
Detroit, Michigan

Albert Kahn Associates, Inc. (AKA), a planning, design and management firm, serves the industrial, health care, higher education, commercial, interiors, R&D technology, urban design, and government markets. The firm provides imaginative solutions that respond to facility-related challenges. With expertise in planning, architecture, and all principal areas of engineering, AKA translates building programs into productive, economical, flexible, and efficient facilities. The demonstrated flexibility and innovation of AKA's teams are a direct result of the freedom to explore ideas, without reservation, and to serve our clients' needs to the fullest extent, enabling us to fulfill our mission statement—"To be our client's first choice."

Anmahian Winton Architects
Cambridge, Massachusetts

Alex Anmahian, AIA, and Nick Winton, AIA, formed Anmahian Winton Architects (AWA) in 1992. Design innovation is the touchstone of the firm's work for residential, institutional, and commercial clients. AWA projects have been featured in numerous publications, including *The New York Times* and *Architectural Record*, and recognized by the Business Week/Architectural Record Award, Architecture Home of the Year Citation, and the AIA Honor Award, among others.

Architecture Research Office
New York, New York

Architecture Research Office believes in an architecture of engagement. The firm's projects—civic, academic, residential, and commercial—connect people with ideas, physical and cultural contexts, and each other. The firm's design process is distinguished by intense inquiry and the active exchange of ideas. Principals Stephen Cassell and Adam Yarinsky founded ARO in 1993. The 16-person practice has been widely recognized with accolades from peer institutions and publications.

Bentel & Bentel, Architects/Planners AIA
Locust Valley, New York

Bentel & Bentel, known for creating inspiring and engaging spaces, has designed more than 250 projects since 1957, from restaurants and residences to religious buildings, public libraries, schools, and universities. The firm has won numerous national and local awards, including two AIA National Honor Awards for the restaurant Craft and St. Stephen Roman Catholic Church, and an AIA/New York City Chapter Design Award for The Modern at MoMA. Bentel & Bentel has 15 staff members specializing in architecture, interior design, and landscape design.

Booth Hansen Associates
Chicago, Illinois

Since 1980, Booth Hansen has helped clients connect people and landscape, while stewarding valuable resources. The firm's work reflects the depth, diversity, and involvement of its clients; employs both innovative and traditional ideas; and creates places with enduring character. In museums and theaters, places of work and places of worship, single-family homes and multifamily residences, renovations and interiors, Booth Hansen aims to enrich the human experience and create architecture of lasting quality.

Cannon Design
Grand Island, New York

Cannon Design is a leading international design firm specializing in health care, higher education, and sports and recreation, as well as public architecture and corporate and commercial projects. With more than 700 staff members delivering services through 14 regional centers, the firm has worked in 42 states and 15 countries in Europe, the Middle East, the Far East, and Latin America.

Chu+Gooding Architects
Los Angeles, California

Chu+Gooding Architects offers distinctive architectural design to institutional, educational, and arts-related clients. Emphasizing design quality, attention to spatial perceptions and materials, and performance, the firm is founded on the belief that a successful environment must be both engaging and useful. The firm integrates architecture, landscape, and interior design, recognizing that all these elements are necessarily interrelated in a well-conceived whole. Chu+Gooding has contributed to more than two dozen projects recognized by national and international architectural publications, and the firm has received more than 30 internationally recognized awards for excellence in design.

Clive Wilkinson Architects
West Hollywood, California

Clive Wilkinson Architects is an architecture and design firm serving creative industries based in Los Angeles. Clive Wilkinson, AIA, established the firm after relocating to the West Coast from London. His background includes 25 years of experience in a wide range of high-profile creative design projects on four continents, most notably in creative office space, entertainment facilities, television stations, and high-tech office development projects. The firm's professional staff members come from many locations and bring an international perspective to their work.

Davis Brody Bond, LLP
New York, New York

Davis Brody Bond develops strong, successful design solutions for complex building types and planning projects for universities, libraries, research laboratories, offices and industrial buildings, health care facilities, housing complexes, and cultural and performing arts centers. This leading architecture practice has a staff of approximately 100 architects, planners, and interior designers who provide services to clients throughout the United States and in 15 countries. The firm has received more than 100 major design awards, including the AIA Firm Award, the highest honor given to an architecture practice, and the 2000 Presidential Design Award for Excellence.

DeStefano+Partners
Chicago, Illinois

DeStefano+Partners is a full-service architecture, urban planning, and interior design practice serving private and public sector clients with a challenging array of design, planning, programming, and assessment needs in new construction and renovation. Respect for context and the broader public realm is a tenet of the firm's practice. The creation of a unique sense of place is a compelling design goal that guides staff members as they shape the physical and conceptual character of a space. Inspired by the cultural, geographic, and organizational diversity of its clientele, the firm's mission is to create environments that are conducive to daily living, supportive of commercial enterprise, and engaging to the human spirit.

Elliott + Associates Architects
Oklahoma City, Oklahoma

The design philosophy of Elliott + Associates Architects stems from the theory that a space reflects the unique personality of the owner and the function it is meant to serve. The firm creates special environments that can be considered architectural portraits of its clients. Each project, like each client, is unique. Key staff members include architects with considerable experience in sustainable design, including use of the U.S. Green Building Council's LEED Green Building Rating System. Lead designer Rand Elliott, FAIA, has a reputation for designing projects that not only fit their sites but also seem to grow from them.

Eskew+Dumez+Ripple
New Orleans, Louisiana

Eskew+Dumez+Ripple is a design-driven studio that produces diverse projects in architecture and planning by blending a signature collaborative process with professional talent, creative thinking, and emerging technologies. The firm creates projects whose authenticity is expressed in their building massing, scale, siting, details, and materials. The firm is committed to enhancing and protecting both the cultural and the natural environments of the communities it serves. Based in New Orleans, the firm uses the cultural and architectural heritage of that city as a platform for a practice of national range. The result is a portfolio that includes aquariums, research laboratories, marine facilities, interpretative centers and museums, as well as office buildings, and academic and health care facilities.

Gabellini Sheppard Associates
New York, New York

Gabellini Sheppard Associates is a multi-disciplinary architectural and interior design firm based in New York City. Founded by Michael Gabellini in 1991, the firm has gained international acclaim for its signature design aesthetic utilizing a simplicity of means relative to form and function.

The 30-person firm designs on multiple scales ranging from intimate residences to urban boutiques and public spaces. Fashion interiors for designers such as Jil Sander, Nicole Farhi, and Giorgio Armani established the firm's facility in using light and space as sculptural materials. Sharing an expertise and passion for contemporary art, Michael Gabellini and Kimberly Sheppard have designed exhibitions for the Solomon R. Guggenheim Museum and galleries such as Marian Goodman Gallery and Anthony Grant Fine Art, among others.

Gabellini Sheppard has been involved with the restoration and renovation of historic buildings in Europe and the United States, including the recently opened Top of the Rock project at 30 Rockefeller Center. The firm has won fifteen awards from the American Institute of Architects on the local, state, and national levels.

Gluckman Mayner Architects
New York, New York

Gluckman Mayner Architects has designed a wide range of institutional, commercial, and residential projects throughout the United States, Europe, and Asia. A major component of the firm's practice has been the design of art-related facilities, and much of the firm's work has grown out of an exchange with artists, curators, and museum directors. Notable projects include the Dia Center for the Arts and the renovation of the Whitney Museum of American Art, both in New York; the Andy Warhol Museum in Pittsburgh; and the Mori Arts Center in Tokyo.

Goettsch Partners (formerly Lohan Associates)
Chicago, Illinois

Goettsch Partners (GP) traces its history to 1938, when Ludwig Mies van der Rohe established his design practice in Chicago. Mies's work in America inspired a new generation of modernists, loosely defined as the Second Chicago School. Today GP, a descendant of Mies's firm, strives for a synthesis of art and craft through construction, for clarity of purpose, and for designs that possess an inspired simplicity.

Group Goetz Architects
Washington, D.C.

Group Goetz Architects (GGA) is a multidisciplinary architecture firm that focuses on renovations and modernizations, interiors, and graphics. GGA believes architecture has a profound effect on the way people live, work, and feel. The firm leverages design to create environments that balance human needs with function, goals, and objectives. GGA approaches design as a strategic tool, employing as a foundation the dynamics that exist among the integrated components of the built environment, which include people, space, technology, materials, building systems, culture, and beauty.

H³ Hardy Collaboration Architecture LLC
New York, New York

H³ Hardy Collaboration Architecture was founded in 2004 by Hugh Hardy and a group of employees from its predecessor firm, Hardy Holzman Pfeiffer Associates.

H³ provides architecture, planning, and interior design services in a flexible, collaborative environment. The firm specializes in projects for performing arts, libraries, educational facilities, residential buildings, museums, commercial office spaces, and restaurants.

From its New York City office the firm have developed a distinctive and successful approach to design that fosters a meaningful dialogue among history, innovation and contemporary use.

Heller Manus Architects
San Francisco, California

Heller Manus Architects has spent 20 years developing a diversified, client-oriented firm that has avoided a singular signature approach. Instead, the firm focuses on finding the ideal design solution for each commission. Projects range from master plans, infill buildings, large- and small-scale retail designs, high-rise office towers, transit shelters, city halls, Beaux-Arts landmark renovations, and streamlined transportation facilities. All projects, however, provide high-quality, cost-effective design that is sensitive to the projects users' function, site, and civic significance.

Herbert Lewis Kruse Blunck Architecture
Des Moines, Iowa

Herbert Lewis Kruse Blunck Architecture is a continuation of the Charles Herbert and Associates architecture firm established in 1961. The firm's collaboration of talents continues their predecessor's excellence in master planning, architectural design, interior design, and landscape architecture—a tradition that has generated some of the region's most significant and enduring buildings. Among other awards, HLKB received the 2001 AIA Firm Award. The firm has produced a body of work noted for its exploration of the possibilities of Modernism. Historian Franz Schulze has remarked that the firm has opened modern architecture "to a variety of avenues hitherto unimagined."

Krueck & Sexton Architects
Chicago, Illinois

Krueck & Sexton Architects is internationally recognized as an innovative and accomplished design firm. Founded in 1979, the firm has produced a body of work noted for its thoughtful and provocative explorations of the possibilities of Modernism. Historian Franz Schulze has remarked that Krueck & Sexton has opened modern architecture "to a variety of avenues hitherto unimagined."

Since its emergence to national attention with A Steel and Glass House in 1981, Krueck & Sexton has developed a design approach characterized by close attention to client need, impeccable detailing, and a dedication to craft. From this beginning, the firm has grown into a full-service practice, offering architecture, interiors, planning, and sustainability.

Lee H. Skolnick Architecture + Design Partnership
New York, New York

Lee H. Skolnick Architecture + Design Partnership is an architecture firm that provides exhibition and museum design services to new and established cultural facilities nationwide. The firm's design methodology focuses on choreographing the visitors' interaction with an exhibit, marrying memory and experience with novel information and situations. This design philosophy encourages visitors to engage in a deep and meaningful exploration and interpretation of the exhibit. The design team prides itself on developing innovative learning environments, and these projects often become major visitor destinations as a result.

McInturff Architects
Bethesda, Maryland

A seven-person firm, McInturff Architects has a diversified client base that includes residential, commercial, and small institutional projects. The firm holds that it is possible to build a viable, vital practice oriented toward the design of small, highly crafted projects and including the entire range of services, from project programming through complete architectural and interior design. Its work has frequently been published, both locally and nationally, and the firm has received more than 200 design awards, including a 2003 AIA Honor Award for Interior Architecture.

Morphosis
Santa Monica, California

With a relatively small staff of 45 designers and architects, Morphosis' objective is to develop a critical practice in which creative output engages the contemporary discourse of the discipline through architectural design and education. The firm won competitions for the CALTRANS District 7 Headquarters in downtown Los Angeles, the NYC2012 Olympic Village, and the Alaska State Capitol Design. Current projects include the NOAA Satellite Control Center in Washington, D.C.; a federal courthouse in Eugene, Oregon; and a social housing project in Madrid, Spain. Morphosis has been honored with awards, and Thom Mayne, FAIA, one of its principals, was the 2005 Pritzker Architecture Prize Laureate, the profession's highest honor.

Pelli Clark Pelli Architects
New Haven, Connecticut

Established in 1977, Pelli Clarke Pelli is a full-service architectural practice of some 80 persons. The firm has worked with corporate, government, and private clients to design major public spaces, museums, airports, laboratories, performing arts centers, academic buildings, hotels, office and residential towers, and mixed-use projects.

The number of commissions the firm accepts is carefully limited to ensure a high degree of personal involvement by the principals. Pelli Clarke Pelli seeks to produce the best possible building for each circumstance. The work of Cesar Pelli is not constrained by a personal style or a signature that would limit his architecture; instead, it tries to celebrate the unique characteristics of each project.

The AIA awarded Pelli Clarke Pelli its 1989 Firm Award in recognition of standard-setting work in architectural design, and in 1995 Cesar Pelli received the Gold Medal from the AIA.

Perkins+Will
Atlanta, Georgia

Founded in 1935, Perkins+Will is a professional service firm staffed with architects, interior designers, and planners. Perkins+Will is a design firm respected both for excellence in design and for service to clients. Through the years, the firm's projects have received hundreds of awards, and its principals have been honored for their contributions to their profession. In 1999, the firm was awarded the AIA Architecture Firm Award, their highest honor. Of equal importance is the firm's adherence to a design process that emphasizes commitment, communication, and coordination, resulting in responsive service and projects that exceed client goals.

Pugh + Scarpa Architecture
Santa Monica, California

Over the last six years Pugh + Scarpa has received 35 major design awards, including nine national AIA Honor Awards, 2005 Record Houses, 2003 Record Interiors, the 2003 Rudy Bruner Prize, and a 2003 AIA COTE Top Ten Green Building Award. In 2004 the Architectural League of New York selected the firm as an emerging voice in architecture. Its work has been exhibited widely, including at the National Building Museum in Washington, D.C.

Robert M. Gurney, FAIA
Alexandria, Virginia

The office of Robert M. Gurney, FAIA, is dedicated to the design of modern, meticulously detailed, thoughtfully ordered residential and commercial projects sensitive to site, program, and budget. Materials are employed with honesty, integrity, and ecological awareness. The design process involves an understanding of site-specific issues of location, landscape, history, availability of materials and construction methods. The office of Robert M. Gurney, FAIA, has won more than ninety design awards and has been published in numerous national and international journals.

Rogers Marvel Architects
Omaha, Nebraska

Rogers Marvel Architects develops project-specific techniques for program analysis and building proposals. Materials, and their means of production and connection, are made evident throughout a project. The staff includes architects, graphic designers, industrial designers, landscape architects, preservationists and digital specialists; their collective skills allow the firm to develop sophisticated buildings and structures, produce master plans, and design parks and urban open spaces.

Shelton, Mindel & Associates
New York, New York

Shelton, Mindel & Associates provides complete architectural, interiors, and product design services for corporate, cultural, academic, retail, recreational, hospitality, and residential clients. The firm is the recipient of numerous AIA awards for interior architecture and seven *Interiors* magazine awards for residential and corporate interiors. Product design lines include collections for Knoll, Waterworks, Jack Lenor Larsen, V'Soske, and Nessen Lighting. *Architectural Digest* has recognized SMA as one of the top 100 design firms of the last century and Peter L. Shelton and Lee F. Mindel, FAIA, as Deans of American Design in 2005.

Skidmore, Owings & Merrill, LLP
Chicago, Illinois

Founded in 1936, Skidmore, Owings & Merrill, LLP (SOM) is one of the largest architecture, urban design and planning, engineering, and interior architecture firms in the United States. The firm's sophistication in building technology applications and commitment to design quality have resulted in a portfolio that features some of the most important architectural accomplishments of the century.

SOM's work ranges from the architectural design and engineering of individual buildings to the master planning and design of entire communities. The firm has conceived, designed, and built projects that include corporate offices, banking, and financial institutions, government buildings, public and private institutions, health care facilities, religious buildings, airports, university buildings, recreational and sports facilities, and residential developments.

Interior architecture was established as an individual discipline at Skidmore, Owings & Merrill, LLP in 1956 to provide clients with interiors services comparable in quality to the firm's architectural services.

Tighe Architecture
Santa Monica, California

Tighe Architecture is committed to creating authentic contemporary design solutions that re-evaluate the way people inhabit their environments. Their work emphasizes process rather than style and is driven by influences from the client, site, budget, culture, society, and the environment. The architecture is a response to the aspirations of the community, a celebration of human activity. The firm was founded in 2000 on the belief that architecture has the power to enhance human life. The firm has won five National AIA Honor Awards.

Trahan Architects
Baton Rouge, Louisiana

Trahan Architects explore the creative use of natural light and materials, utilizing the environment to celebrate man's relationship with nature and create a sense of community that is both comforting and challenging. With an emphasis on creative vision aimed to enhance a program's purpose and concern for building quality, Trahan Architects have been recognized throughout the world for their fresh approach to creating space.

Trahan Architects has participated in several competitions, receiving first prize in three invited international design competitions based in Beijing, China. The emphasis the firm gives to design is complemented by Trahan Architect's proficiency in a wide range of project types. Completed and active projects include ecclesiastical, financial, academic, and sports stadia designs.

Turnbull Griffin Haesloop
San Francisco, California

The female-owned firm of Turnbull Griffin Haesloop is known for its design of houses, as well as wineries, churches, independent schools, and civic complexes. The firm's 12 architecture and design professionals believe architecture is primarily concerned with establishing a sense of place, inspired by the uniqueness of each site and each client. Since its building design concepts are rooted in the environment of the projects, the firm is particularly attentive to topography, microclimate, and vegetation.

Valerio Dewalt Train Associates, Inc.
Chicago, Illinois

Valerio Dewalt Train Associates, Inc., a national architectural practice based in Chicago, combines strengths in design, innovation, project management, and vision to provide high-value design services to a demanding clientele that includes leading developers, corporations, foundations, and cultural institutions. The firm of nearly 50 architects is known for its high-energy design, and its work has received numerous design awards and has been published in every major international design journal.

WalkerGroup/CNI
Los Angeles, California

WalkerGroup creates unique design solutions to serve its clients. At the core of its practice the firm combines and contrasts different approaches to creating designs. Powerful architectural forms contrast with memorable graphic design. Expansive strategies and concepts guide technical documentation and construction detailing. Master planning contrasts with elegant package design. The firm combines the resources of an international firm with attention to detail and hands-on care.

Weiss/Manfredi
New York, New York

Weiss/Manfredi Architecture/ Landscape/Urbanism is a multidisciplinary design practice based in New York. Founded by Marion Weiss and Michael Manfredi, the firm is known for their integration of architecture, art, infrastructure, and landscape design. They were awarded the Academy Award for Architecture by the American Academy of Arts and Letters, and were named "an emerging voice" by the Architectural League of New York. Interdisciplinary projects such as their competition-winning Seattle Art Museum Olympic Sculpture Park have been exhibited at the Museum of Modern Art, Harvard University, and the Design Center in Essen, Germany. They are currently working on the Nexus, a multi-use arts building in New York. The firm has won numerous awards including national and international design competitions and has been featured in national and international publications and exhibitions including the Museum of Modern Art, the Venice Architectural Biennale, the Sao Paolo Biennale of International Architecture and Design, the Cooper-Hewitt Museum's Design Culture Now Triennial, and the National Building Museum.

William Kite Architects, Inc.
Providence, Rhode Island

William Kite Architects is a ten-person Rhode Island-based firm. The practice exemplifies a rigorous, but humanistic, approach to the design process, creating buildings and spaces that relate and speak to the people who use them. KITE believes that design and technical issues must be treated equally and that architecture should be fun, both in the process and in the result.

William Rawn Associates, Architects, Inc.
Boston, Massachusetts

Formed in 1983, William Rawn Associates is committed to buildings participating in the civic or public realm. The form believes that successful architecture, through the active engagement of its civic context, fosters the values of diversity, meritocracy, and participation that are fundamental to the American democratic experience. William Rawn Associates has completed a large number of project ranging from complex urban buildings to college campuses, from performing arts facilities to affordable housing. Best known is the 1,200-seat Seiji Ozawa Hall for the Boston Symphony Orchestra at Tanglewood, and recently completed projects include an overall campus Master Plan and architectural design of the West Campus mixed-use precinct at Northeastern University in Boston and the Music Center at Strathmore in Montgomery County, Maryland, the second home of the Baltimore Symphony Orchestra.

Photography Credits